21ST CENTURY

EXCLUSIVE DISTRIBUTORS:
MUSIC SALES LIMITED
8/9 FRITH STREET, LONDON W1D 3JB,
ENGLAND.
MUSIC SALES PTY LIMITED
120 ROTHSCHILD AVENUE, ROSEBERY,
NSW 2018, AUSTRALIA.

ORDER NO. AM968737
ISBN 0-7119-8654-1
THIS BOOK © COPYRIGHT 2002
BY WISE PUBLICATIONS.

COMPILED BY NICK CRISPIN.
MUSIC ARRANGED BY RIKKY ROOKSBY.
MUSIC PROCESSED BY THE PITTS.

COVER DESIGN BY PHIL GAMBRILL.
PRINTED IN THE UNITED KINGDOM BY
CALIGRAVING LIMITED, THETFORD, NORFOLK.

YOUR GUARANTEE OF QUALITY:
AS PUBLISHERS, WE STRIVE TO PRODUCE EVERY
BOOK TO THE HIGHEST COMMERCIAL STANDARDS.
THE MUSIC HAS BEEN FRESHLY ENGRAVED AND
THE BOOK HAS BEEN CAREFULLY DESIGNED
TO MINIMISE AWKWARD PAGE TURNS AND TO
MAKE PLAYING FROM IT A REAL PLEASURE.
PARTICULAR CARE HAS BEEN GIVEN TO
SPECIFYING ACID-FREE, NEUTRAL-SIZED
PAPER MADE FROM PULPS WHICH HAVE
NOT BEEN ELEMENTAL CHLORINE BLEACHED.
THIS PULP IS FROM FARMED SUSTAINABLE
FORESTS AND WAS PRODUCED WITH
SPECIAL REGARD FOR THE ENVIRONMENT.
THROUGHOUT, THE PRINTING AND BINDING HAVE
BEEN PLANNED TO ENSURE A STURDY,
ATTRACTIVE PUBLICATION WHICH
SHOULD GIVE YEARS OF ENJOYMENT.
IF YOUR COPY FAILS TO MEET OUR HIGH STANDARDS,
PLEASE INFORM US AND WE WILL GLADLY REPLACE IT.

MUSIC SALES' COMPLETE CATALOGUE DESCRIBES
THOUSANDS OF TITLES AND IS AVAILABLE IN FULL COLOUR
SECTIONS BY SUBJECT, DIRECT FROM MUSIC SALES LIMITED.
PLEASE STATE YOUR AREAS OF INTEREST AND SEND
A CHEQUE/POSTAL ORDER FOR £1.50 FOR POSTAGE TO:
MUSIC SALES LIMITED, NEWMARKET ROAD,
BURY ST. EDMUNDS, SUFFOLK IP33 3YB.

WWW.MUSICSALES.COM

WISE PUBLICATIONS
LONDON / NEW YORK / PARIS / SYDNEY / COPENHAGEN / BERLIN / MADRID / TOKYO

Relative Tuning

The guitar can be tuned with the aid of pitch pipes or dedicated electronic guitar tuners which are available through your local music dealer. If you do not have a tuning device, you can use relative tuning. Estimate the pitch of the 6th string as near as possible to E or at least a comfortable pitch (not too high, as you might break other strings in tuning up). Then, while checking the various positions on the diagram, place a finger from your left hand on the:

5th fret of the E or 6th string and **tune the open A** (or 5th string) to the note Ⓐ

5th fret of the A or 5th string and **tune the open D** (or 4th string) to the note Ⓓ

5th fret of the D or 4th string and **tune the open G** (or 3rd string) to the note Ⓖ

4th fret of the G or 3rd string and **tune the open B** (or 2nd string) to the note Ⓑ

5th fret of the B or 2nd string and **tune the open E** (or 1st string) to the note Ⓔ

E	A	D	G	B	E
or	or	or	or	or	or
6th	5th	4th	3rd	2nd	1st

Head

Nut

1st Fret

2nd Fret

3rd Fret

4th Fret

5th Fret

Reading Chord Boxes

Chord boxes are diagrams of the guitar neck viewed head upwards, face on as illustrated. The top horizontal line is the nut, unless a higher fret number is indicated, the others are the frets.

The vertical lines are the strings, starting from E (or 6th) on the left to E (or 1st) on the right.

The black dots indicate where to place your fingers.

Strings marked with an O are played open, not fretted. Strings marked with an X should not be played.

The curved bracket indicates a 'barre' – hold down the s under the bracket with your first finger, using your fingers to fret the remaining notes.

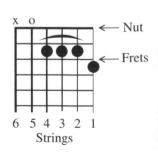

x   o

← Nut

← Frets

6 5 4 3 2 1
Strings

ANDROGYNY

WORDS & MUSIC BY SHIRLEY MANSON, BUTCH VIG, DUKE ERIKSON & STEVE MARKER

Am   Dm   F   Em   D   G

C   E♭   Fm   A♭   A♭m7   F7

Intro | Am   Dm | F   Em | Am   Dm | F   Em ‖

Verse 1

Am   Dm
When everything is going wrong

        F   Em
And you can't see the point in going on,

Am   Dm
Nothing in life is set in stone,

      F   Em
There's nothing that can't be turned around.

Am   Dm
Nobody wants to feel alone.

F   Em
Everybody wants to love someone.

Am   Dm
Out of the tree go pick a plum.

F   Em
Why can't we all just get along?

Link 1 | F | D | (Em)   ‖

On,_____   on,_____

Chorus 1

Em
(Boys) Boys in the girls' room,

  G
(Girls) Girls in the men's room,

C   Em
    You free your mind in your androgyny.

cont.

G
(Boys) Boys in the parlour,

C
(Girls) They're getting harder.

F   N.C.
  I'll free your mind and your androgyny.

Verse 2

    Am   Dm
No sweeter a taste that you could find

     F   Em
Than fruit hanging ripe upon the vine.

      Am   Dm
There's never been an oyster so divine,

F   Em
  A river deep that never runs dry.

Link 2 | Am Dm | F   Em | Am Dm | F   Em ‖

Verse 3

    Am   Dm
The birds and the bees they hum along,

     F   Em
Like treasure they twinkle in the sun.

Am   Dm
  Get on board and have some fun,

F   Em
Take what you need to turn you on.

Link 3 | F | D   ‖
              On,____

Chorus 2

Em
(Boys) Boys in the girls' room,

 G
(Girls) Girls in the men's room,

C   Em
  You free your mind in your androgyny.

 G
(Boys) Boys in the parlour,

 C
(Girls) They're getting harder.

F
  I'll free your mind, I'll free your mind,

I'll free your mind, I'll free your…

Bridge

E♭   Fm   A♭
(Boys) Behind closed doors and under stars, (girls)

       A♭m7   E♭
It doesn't matter where you are, (boys)

     Fm   A♭
Collecting jewels that catch your eye, (girls)

     A♭m7   N.C.   F7
Don't let a soulmate pass you   by.

Chorus 3

Em
   Boys in the girls' room,

G
   Girls in the men's room,

C   Em
   You free your mind in your androgyny.

G
   Boys in the parlour,

C
   They're getting harder.

F   G
   I'll free your mind, I'll free your mind.

Chorus 4

G
Boys in the girls' room,

C
Girls in the men's room,

F   Em
You free your mind in your androgyny.

G
   Boys in the parlour,

C
   They're getting harder;

F
   I'll free your mind, I'll free your mind,

I'll free your mind, I'll free your…

Coda

G   C   F   G
Boys, girls, boys, girls.

ALL THE SMALL THINGS

WORDS & MUSIC BY MARK HOPPUS & THOMAS DELONGE

G   F   C   Csus⁴

Intro   G F ‖: C | Csus⁴ | G | G F :‖

Verse 1

    C   G   F
All the   small things,

           G   C
True care, truth brings.

           G   F
I'll take   one lift,

           G
Your ride, best trip.

    C   G   F
    Always I know

          G   C
You'll be at my show

          G   F   G
Watching, waiting, commiserating.

    C   (G)
    Say it ain't so, I will not go,

                  (F)
Turn the lights off, carry me (home.)

Chorus 1

    C
Na, na, na, na, na na, na na na na.
home.

    G   F
Na, na, na, na, na na, na na na na.

    C
Na, na, na, na, na na, na na na na.

    G   F
Na, na, na, na, na na, na na na na.

Link   ‖: C | Csus⁴ C | G | G F :‖

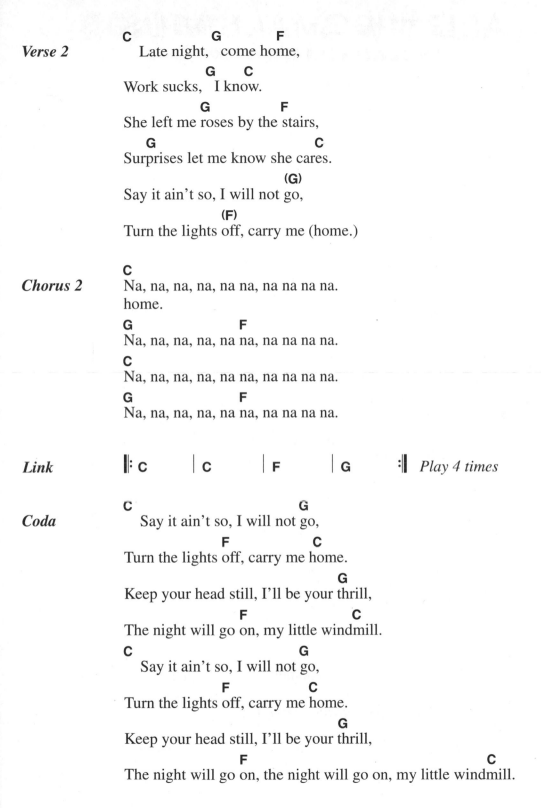

Verse 2

    C   G   F
    Late night,   come home,

           G   C
Work sucks,   I know.

          G   F
She left me roses by the stairs,

      G   C
Surprises let me know she cares.

                        (G)
Say it ain't so, I will not go,

               (F)
Turn the lights off, carry me (home.)

Chorus 2

C
Na, na, na, na, na na, na na na na.
home.

G   F
Na, na, na, na, na na, na na na na.

C
Na, na, na, na, na na, na na na na.

G   F
Na, na, na, na, na na, na na na na.

Link   ‖: C | C | F | G   :‖ *Play 4 times*

Coda

    C   G
    Say it ain't so, I will not go,

                F   C
Turn the lights off, carry me home.

                          G
Keep your head still, I'll be your thrill,

                F   C
The night will go on, my little windmill.

C   G
    Say it ain't so, I will not go,

                F   C
Turn the lights off, carry me home.

                          G
Keep your head still, I'll be your thrill,

                F   C
The night will go on, the night will go on, my little windmill.

BETWEEN ANGELS AND INSECTS

WORDS & MUSIC BY PAPA ROACH

Dm   B♭   F/A   C   Am   F   E♭   fr3

Intro | Dm | B♭ | F/A | C ‖

Chorus 1
Dm   B♭
   There's no money,   there's no possessions,
F/A   C
   Only obsession,   I don't need that shit,
Dm
   Take my money, take my obsession.

Link 1 | Dm C | Dm C | Am C | Am C |

| Dm C | Dm C | Am B♭ | F E♭ ‖

Verse 1
                 Dm
I just want to be heard, loud and clear are my words,
F
Coming from within, man, tell them what you heard:
Am   B♭
   It's about a revolution, in your heart and in your mind,
C
Till you find a conclusion,
Dm
   Lost out in obsession,
        F
Diamond rings get you nothing but a life-long lesson,
Am
   And your pocketbook's stressing
       B♭   C
You're a slave to the system, working jobs that you hate
Dm
   For that shit you don't need.

          F   **Am**
It's too bad the world is based on greed,   step back and see,
B♭   **C**
Stop thinking about yourself, start thinking about:

Chorus 2

    Dm   **C** **Dm**   **C**
   There's no money,   there's no possession,
Am   **C**   **Am**   **C**
   Only obsession, I don't need that shit.
Dm   **C** **Dm**   **C**
   Take my money, take my possession,
Am   **C**   **Am**   **C**
   Take my obsession, I don't need that… (shit)

Verse 2

                                        Dm
Because everything is nothing, and emptiness isn't everything,
F
   This reality is really just a fucked-up dream,
Am
   With the flesh and the blood that you call your soul,
B♭   **C**
   Flip it inside out, it's a big black hole.
Dm
   Take your money, burn it up like an asteroid,
F
   Possession, though you're never gonna fill the void.
Am
   Take it away and learn your best lesson,
     B♭   **C**
The heart, the soul, the life, the passion.

Chorus 3   As Chorus 2

Bridge

Dm   **B♭**   **F/A**
   Money, possession, ____
             C
Obsession.

Link 2 | **Dm** | **B♭** | **F/A** | **C**   ‖

Verse 3

```
      Dm                B♭              F/A
      Present yourself,   press your clothes,
                      C
      Comb your hair   and clock in.
      Dm                B♭              F/A
      You just can't win,   just can't win,
                              C            Dm
      And the things you own,    own you. No!_____
```

Chorus 4

```
      Dm          C    Dm          C
      Take my money,   take my possession,
      Am        C       Am          C
      Take my obsession,  I don't need   that shit.
      Dm          C    Dm          C
      Fuck your money,   fuck your possession,
      Am          C       Am          C
      Fuck your obsession,  I don't need   that shit.
      Dm   C   Dm   C        Am   C
      Money,   possession,    obsession,
      Am          C       Dm
      I don't need   that shit.
```

BOHEMIAN LIKE YOU

WORDS & MUSIC BY COURTNEY TAYLOR-TAYLOR

Intro
‖: (B) | (D) | (A) | (E)   :‖

‖: B Bsus4 B | D Dsus4 D | A Asus4 A | E Esus4 E :‖

| B E5 | B E5 | B E5 ‖

Verse 1

B G

You've got a great car,

D B

Yeah, what's wrong with it today?

A E

I used to have one too,

E C

Maybe I'll come and have a look.

B G   D

I really love your hairdo, yeah,

A

I'm glad you like mine too.

E

See, we're looking pretty cool.

Getcha.

Link 1
| B E5 | B E5 | B E5 ‖

Verse 2

       B   E5   B
So what do you do?

          D
Oh yeah, I wait tables too.

    A
No, I haven't heard your band

        E
'Cause you guys are pretty new.

       B   D
But if you dig on vegan food

       A
Well, come over to my work,

        E
I'll have them cook you something

          B
That you really love.

Chorus 1

        D   A
'Cause I like you, yeah I like you,

       E   B
And I'm feeling so bohemian like you.

        D   A
Yeah I like you, yeah I like you,

      E
And I feel wa-ho, whoo!

Link 2

‖: B Bsus4 B | D Dsus4 D | A Asus4 A | E Esus4 E :‖

| B   E5 | B   E5 | B   E5 | B   ‖
                                    Wait!

Verse 3

N.C.   B   D
Who's that guy just hanging at your pad?

     A
He's looking kind of bummed.

       E
Yeah, you broke up? That's too bad.

       B   D
I guess it's fair if he always pays the rent

     A
And he doesn't get bent about

E   B
Sleeping on the couch when I'm there.

Chorus 2

      D   A
'Cause I like you, yeah I like you,

        E   B
And I'm feeling so bohemian like you.

      D   A
Yeah I like you, yeah I like you,

       E
And I feel wa-ho, whoo!

Link 3   ‖: B Bsus⁴ B | D Dsus⁴ D | A Asus⁴ A | E Esus⁴ E :‖

Chorus 3

      B
And I'm getting wise

      D   A
And I feel so bohemian like you.

       E
It's you that I want

       B   D   A
So please, just a casual, casual easy thing.

E   B
Is it? It is for me.

       D   A   E
And I like you, yeah I like you, and I like you, I like you,

     B   D   A
 I like you, I like you, I like you, I like you, I like you

      E
And I feel who-hoa, whoo!

Coda   ‖: B Bsus⁴ B | D Dsus⁴ D | A Asus⁴ A | E Esus⁴ E :‖

       | B E⁵ | B E⁵ | B E⁵ | B E⁵ | B   ‖

BLISS

LYRICS & MUSIC BY MATTHEW BELLAMY

Cm   Bb   Fm   C   Am   C/G   E

Intro

‖: Cm | Bb | Fm | Cm |

| Bb | Fm | Cm | Cm :‖

Verse 1

Cm   Bb   Fm   Cm
    Ev'rything about you is how I'd wanna be,
    Bb   Fm   Cm
Your freedom comes naturally.
            Bb   Fm   Cm
Ev'rything about you resonates happiness,
        Bb   Fm   Cm
Now I won't settle   for less.

Chorus 1

C Am   C/G   C   Am   E   Fm
    Give me   all the peace and joy in your mind. Ooh___

Link 1

| Cm | Bb | Fm | Cm |

| Bb | Fm | Cm | Cm ‖

Verse 2

Cm   Bb   Fm   Cm
    Ev'rything about you pains my envying,
    Bb   Fm   Cm
Your soul can't hate anything.
            Bb   Fm   Cm
Ev'rything about you is so easy to love,
        Bb   Fm   Cm
They're watching you from above.

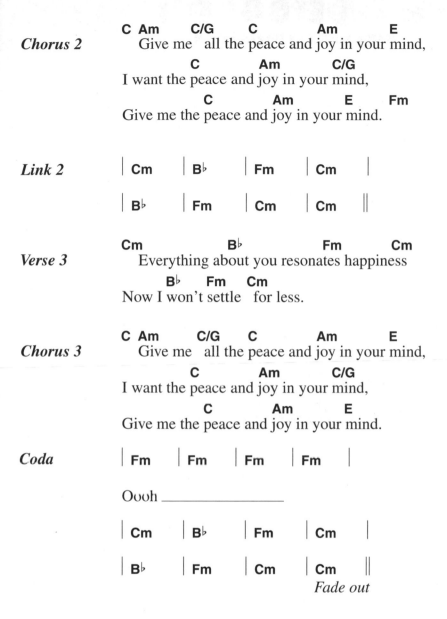

Chorus 2

C Am   C/G   C   Am   E
Give me   all the peace and joy in your mind,

             C   Am   C/G
I want the peace and joy in your mind,

                C   Am   E   Fm
Give me the peace and joy in your mind.

Link 2

| Cm | Bb | Fm | Cm |

| Bb | Fm | Cm | Cm ||

Verse 3

Cm   Bb   Fm   Cm
Everything about you resonates happiness

      Bb   Fm   Cm
Now I won't settle   for less.

Chorus 3

C Am   C/G   C   Am   E
Give me   all the peace and joy in your mind,

             C   Am   C/G
I want the peace and joy in your mind,

                C   Am   E
Give me the peace and joy in your mind.

Coda

| Fm | Fm | Fm | Fm |

Oooh _____

| Cm | Bb | Fm | Cm |

| Bb | Fm | Cm | Cm ||

Fade out

15

BUCK ROGERS

WORDS & MUSIC BY GRANT NICHOLAS

Tune guitar slightly flat

Intro | F | F A5 B♭5 | F | F A5 B♭5 ||

Verse 1

F5   A5   B♭5   F5 A5   B♭5 F5
    He's got a brand new car, looks like a jaguar,

A5   B♭5 F5 A5   B♭5 F   A5   B♭5
It's got leather seats, it's got a CD player.

| F | F A5 B♭5 |

C   B♭
    But I don't wanna talk about it anymore.

Chorus 1

N.C.   F
I think we're gonna make it,

C   Dm   B♭
    I think we're gonna save it, ye - ah,

             F
So don't you try and fake it,

C   B♭
    Anymore, anymore.

Link 1 | F | F A5 B♭5 | F | F A5 B♭5 ||

Verse 2

F5   A5   B♭5 F5 A5   B♭5   F5
    We'll start over again,   grow ourselves new skin;

A5   B♭5   F5   A5   B♭5   F   A5   B♭5
Get a house in Devon,   drink cider from a lemon.

| F | F A5 B♭5 |

C   B♭
    But I don't wanna talk about it anymore.

Chorus 2   As Chorus 1

Chorus 3

B♭   **F**
I think we're gonna make it,

C   **Dm**   **B♭**
  I think we're gonna save it, ye - ah,

           F
So don't you try and fake it,

C   **B♭**
  Anymore, anymore.

Bridge

G5 **A5** **B♭5**   **D♭5**   **G5** **A5** **B♭5**
           He's got a brand new car,

           F5
He's got a brand new car,

A brand new car, a brand new car, a brand new car.

Link 2 | **F5** | **F5** | **A5** **B♭5** | **F5** |

Chorus 4

A5 **B♭5**   **F**
    I think we're gonna make it,

C   **Dm**   **B♭**
  I think we're gonna save it, ye - ah,

           F
So don't you try and fake it,

C   **B♭**
  Anymore, anymore.

Chorus 5

B♭   **F**
I think we're gonna make it,

C   **Dm**   **B♭**
  I think we're gonna save it, ye - ah,

           F
So don't you try and fake it,

C   **B♭**
  Anymore, anymore.

Coda | **F** | **F A5** **B♭5** ‖

CHOP SUEY!

WORDS BY SERJ TANKIAN & DARON MALAKIAN. MUSIC BY DARON MALAKIAN

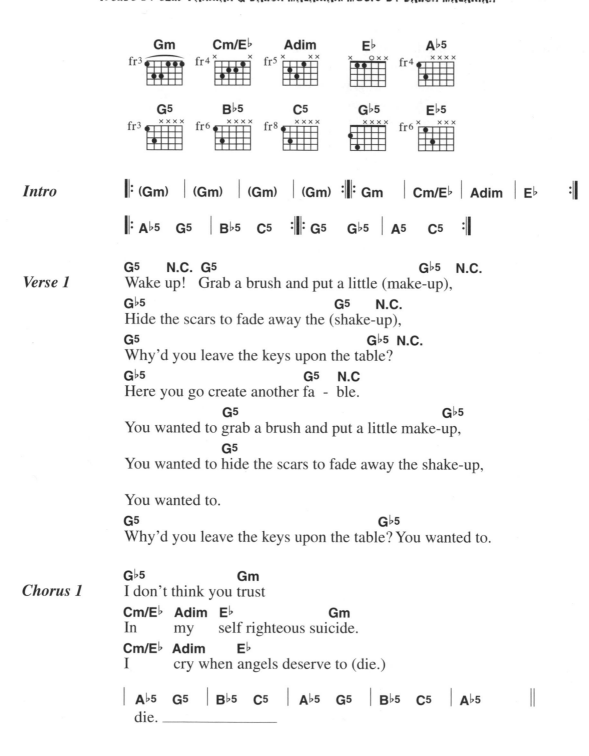

Intro

‖: (Gm) | (Gm) | (Gm) | (Gm) :‖: Gm | Cm/E♭ | Adim | E♭ :‖

‖: A♭5 G5 | B♭5 C5 :‖: G5 G♭5 | A5 C5 :‖

Verse 1

G5   N.C. G5   G♭5   N.C.
Wake up!   Grab a brush and put a little (make-up),

G♭5   G5   N.C.
Hide the scars to fade away the (shake-up),

G5   G♭5 N.C.
Why'd you leave the keys upon the table?

G♭5   G5   N.C
Here you go create another fa - ble.

                    G5   G♭5
You wanted to grab a brush and put a little make-up,

                    G5
You wanted to hide the scars to fade away the shake-up,

You wanted to.

G5   G♭5
Why'd you leave the keys upon the table? You wanted to.

Chorus 1

G♭5   Gm
I don't think you trust

Cm/E♭ Adim E♭   Gm
In   my   self righteous suicide.

Cm/E♭ Adim   E♭
I   cry when angels deserve to (die.)

| A♭5 G5 | B♭5 C5 | A♭5 G5 | B♭5 C5 | A♭5 ‖
die. _____

Verse 2   As Verse 1

Chorus 2
G♭5   Gm
I don't think you trust

Cm/E♭ Adim E♭   Gm
In   my   self righteous suicide.

Cm/E♭ Adim   E♭   Gm
I   cry when angels deserve to die. ____

Chorus 3
Cm/E♭ Adim E♭   Gm
In   my   self righteous suicide.

Cm/E♭ Adim   E♭
I   cry when angels deserve to die.

| A♭5 G5 | B♭5 C5 | A♭5 G5 | B♭5 C5 ‖

Coda
A♭5   G5   B♭5   C5
Father, Father, Father, Father,

A♭5   G5   B♭5   C5
Father, Father, Father, Father,

G5   G♭5   A5   C5
Father into your hands   I commend my spirit.

G5   G♭5
    Father into your hands…

A5   C5   Gm
Why have you forsaken me?

E♭5   B♭5
In your eyes forsaken me?

E♭5   Gm
In your thoughts forsaken me?

E♭5   B♭5   E♭5
In your heart forsaken me?

Gm E♭5 B♭5 E♭5   Gm
Trust in   my   self-righteous suicide.

E♭5 B♭5   E♭5   Gm
I   cry when angels deserve to die.

E♭5 B♭5 E♭5   Gm
In   my   self-righteous suicide.

E♭5 B♭5   E♭5   Gm
I   cry when angels deserve to die.

CRAWLING

WORDS & MUSIC BY CHESTER BENNINGTON, ROB BOURDON, BRAD DELSON, JOSEPH HAHN & MIKE SHINODA

C#m   Amaj7   B   E   C#   Aadd9

Intro

| C#m | C#m | Amaj7 | Amaj7 |

| Amaj7 | B | C#m | E ||

Chorus 1

C#   Aadd9   E   B
Crawling in my skin, these wounds they will not heal.

C#   Aadd9   E   B
Fear is how I fall, confusing what is real. _____

Link

| C#m | Amaj7 | E | B ||

Verse 1

C#m   Amaj7
  There's something inside me that pulls beneath the surface,

E   B
  Consuming,   confusing,

C#m   Amaj7
  This lack of self-control I fear is never ending,

E   B   Amaj7   B
  Controlling,   I can't seem _____ to find myself again,

                C#m
My walls are closing in,

(Without a sense of self confidence,

    E   Amaj7
I'm convinced that there's just too much pressure to take),

           B
I've felt this way before,

       C#m   E
So insecure. _____

Chorus 2   As Chorus 1

Verse 2

C#m   Amaj7
 Discomfort endlessly has pulled itself upon me,

E   B
 Distracting, reacting.

C#m   Amaj7
 Against my will I stand beside my own reflection,

E   B   Amaj7
 It's haunting how I can't seem _____

        B
To find myself again,

         C#m
My walls are closing in,

(Without a sense of confidence,

  E   Amaj7
I'm convinced that there's just too much pressure to take),

       B
I've felt this way before,

     C#m E | E |
So insecure. _____

Chorus 3   As Chorus 1

Chorus 4

C#   Aadd9 E   B
Crawling in my skin, these wounds they will not heal.

C#   Aadd9 E   B   C#m
Fear is how I fall, confusing, confusing what is real. _____

Coda

               Amaj7
(There's something inside me that pulls beneath the surface,

E   B   C#m
 Consuming), confusing what is real.

         Amaj7   E
(This lack of self-control I fear is never ending, controlling),

   B
Confusing what is real.

THE CRYSTAL LAKE

WORDS & MUSIC BY JASON LYTLE

C   F   Am   Fm

D♯dim   Dm   G   B♭   A♭   fr4

Intro | C | C | F | F | Am | Am |

F
Should never have left the crystal lake.

| C | C | Fm | Fm | Am | Am | Fm | Fm   ‖

Verse 1
C
Should never have left the crystal lake
D♯dim
For parties full of folks who flake.
Dm
Italian leather, winter games,
Fm   G
Retired by the duraflames.

Verse 2
C
The crystal lake, it only laughs,
D♯dim
It knows you're just a modern man.
Dm
It's shining like a chandelier,
Fm   B♭
Shining somewhere far away from here.

Chorus 1

B♭   A♭
   I've gotta get out of here,

B♭   A♭
   I've gotta get out of here,

B♭   A♭
   I've gotta get out of here,

B♭   A♭   Fm
   I've gotta get out of here ____

G   N.C.   (A♭)
   And find my way again,

N.C.
I've lost my way a - (gain.)

Link

| C | C | Fm | Fm | Am | Am | |

- gain.

        Fm
Should never have left the crystal lake.

| C | C | Fm | Fm | Am | Am | Fm | Fm ‖

Verse 3

        C
Should never have left the crystal lake,

      D♯dim
For areas where trees are fake,

      Dm
And dogs are dead with broken hearts,

     Fm   G
Collapsing by the coffee carts.

Verse 4   As Verse 2

Chorus 2   As Chorus 1

Coda

| C | C | Fm | Fm | C | C | |

        Fm
Should never have left the crystal lake.

‖: C | C | Fm | Fm :‖ C | ‖

Play 8 times

(DRAWING) RINGS AROUND THE WORLD

WORDS & MUSIC BY GRUFF RHYS, DAFYDD IEUAN, GUTO PRYCE, HUW BUNFORD & CIAN CIARAN

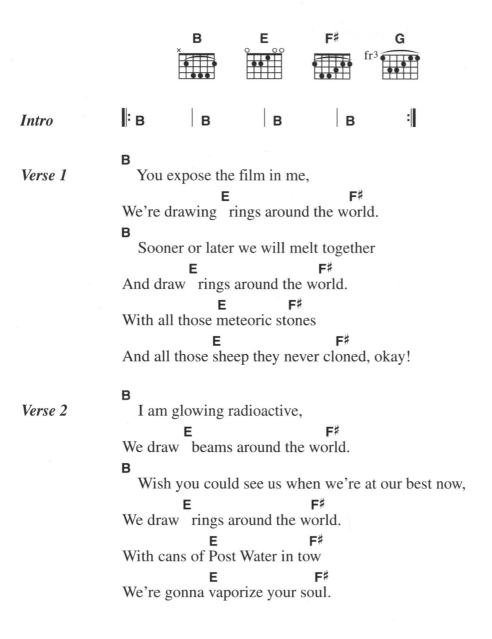

Intro ‖: B | B | B | B :‖

Verse 1

B
    You expose the film in me,
           E   F♯
We're drawing rings around the world.
B
    Sooner or later we will melt together
         E   F♯
And draw rings around the world.
         E   F♯
With all those meteoric stones
         E   F♯
And all those sheep they never cloned, okay!

Verse 2

B
    I am glowing radioactive,
        E   F♯
We draw beams around the world.
B
    Wish you could see us when we're at our best now,
        E   F♯
We draw rings around the world.
        E   F♯
With cans of Post Water in tow
        E   F♯
We're gonna vaporize your soul.

Verse 3

B
   Earth will become Saturn II
        E   F♯
With all the   rings around the world.
B
   Tetsuo II became me and you
           E   F♯
With all those   rings around the world,
          E   F♯
And all those body hammer-blows,
             E   F♯
We're drawing rings around the world. Ha-ha!

Chorus

‖: B
    Ring, ring! Ring, ring!
G   F♯
Rings around the world. :‖ *Play 6 times*
B
Ring, ring! Ring, ring!
G   F♯
Rings around the world.

Coda

‖: (B) | (B) | (G) | (F♯)   :‖ *Repeat to fade*
                                                  with sound effects

BURN BABY BURN

WORDS & MUSIC BY TIM WHEELER

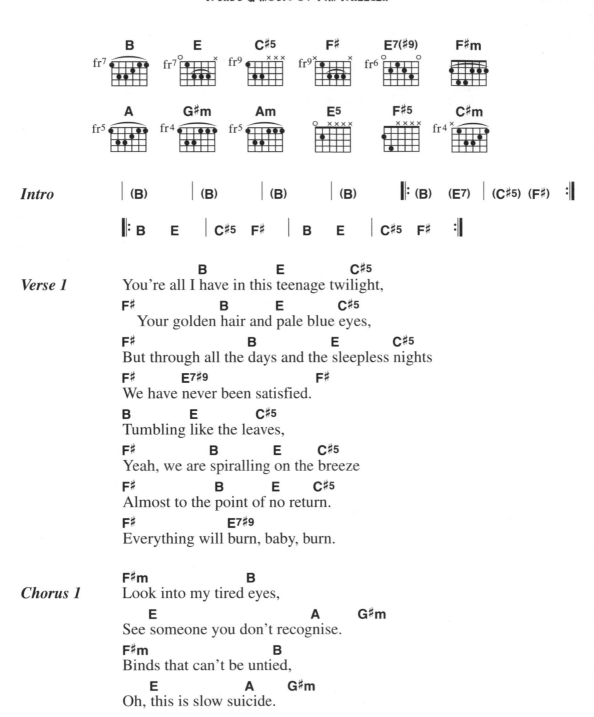

Intro | (B) | (B) | (B) | (B) ‖: (B) (E7) | (C#5) (F#) :‖

‖: B E | C#5 F# | B E | C#5 F# :‖

Verse 1

            B   E   C#5
You're all I have in this teenage twilight,

F#   B   E   C#5
  Your golden hair and pale blue eyes,

F#   B   E   C#5
But through all the days and the sleepless nights

F#   E7#9   F#
We have never been satisfied.

B   E   C#5
Tumbling like the leaves,

F#   B   E   C#5
Yeah, we are spiralling on the breeze

F#   B   E   C#5
Almost to the point of no return.

F#   E7#9
Everything will burn, baby, burn.

Chorus 1

F#m   B
Look into my tired eyes,

     E   A   G#m
See someone you don't recognise.

F#m   B
Binds that can't be untied,

     E   A   G#m
Oh, this is slow suicide.

cont.

```
     F♯m      N.C.              B
     Feelings that I can't disguise
              E                A
     And never will be reconciled.
     G♯m  F♯m                B      Am
     Oh,   something inside has died.
```

Link

```
     ‖: B    E    | C♯5  F♯   :‖
```

Verse 2

```
          B         E         C♯5
     You walk like you're in a daze,
     F♯          B        E      C♯5
     Unresponsive eyes in a distant gaze,
     F♯          B              E      C♯5
     Like all the good times have flown away
     F♯            E7♯9                     F♯
     And their memory leaves a bitter taste.
     B         E        C♯5
     Tumbling like the leaves,
     F♯           B         E     C♯5
     Yeah, we are spiralling on the breeze,
          F♯   B    E     C♯5
     Destructive love is all we have,
          F♯    E7♯9
     Destructive love is all I am.
```

Chorus 2

```
     F♯m                  B
     Look into my tired eyes,
           E                    A       G♯m
     See someone you don't recognise.
     F♯m                  B
     Binds that can't be untied,
           E           A     G♯m
     Oh, this is slow suicide.
     F♯m      N.C.              B
     Feelings that I can't disguise
              E                A
     And never will be reconciled.
          F♯m                B      Am
     Oh, something inside has died.
```

Solo

```
     ‖: B    E    | C♯5  F♯   | B    E    | C♯5  F♯   :‖
```

27

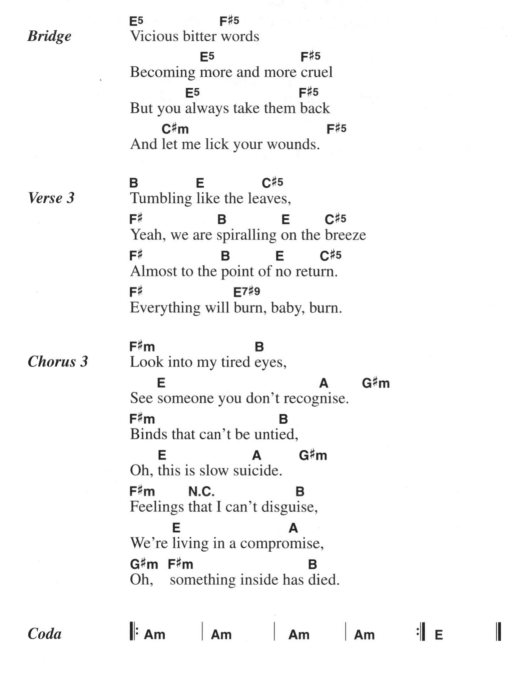

Bridge

E5   F#5
Vicious bitter words
            E5   F#5
Becoming more and more cruel
           E5   F#5
But you always take them back
      C#m   F#5
And let me lick your wounds.

Verse 3

B   E   C#5
Tumbling like the leaves,
F#   B   E   C#5
Yeah, we are spiralling on the breeze
F#   B   E   C#5
Almost to the point of no return.
F#   E7#9
Everything will burn, baby, burn.

Chorus 3

F#m   B
Look into my tired eyes,
      E   A   G#m
See someone you don't recognise.
F#m   B
Binds that can't be untied,
      E   A   G#m
Oh, this is slow suicide.
F#m   N.C.   B
Feelings that I can't disguise,
      E   A
We're living in a compromise,
G#m F#m   B
Oh,   something inside has died.

Coda   ‖: Am | Am | Am | Am   :‖ E   ‖

FAT LIP

WORDS & MUSIC BY GREIG NORI, DERYCK WHIBLEY, STEVE JOCZ & DAVE BAKSH

E   A   B   C#m   G#   B/D#   D

Intro

‖: (E) | (E) | (E) | (E) :‖: E | E A | E | E A :‖

Verse 1

```
        E                                          B
Storming through the party like my name was El Niño,
            A
Well I was hanging out, drinking in the back of an El Camino.
        E                               B
As a kid, was a skid, no-one knew me by name,
            A
Trashed my own house party 'cause nobody came.
          E
I know I'm not the one you thought you knew back in high school,
C#m                           A
Never going, never showing up when we had to.
          E
It's attention that we crave, don't tell us to behave,
        C#m                          A
I'm sick of always hearing  "Act your age".
```

Chorus 1

```
                E     B  C#m
I don't wanna waste my time,
                  G#   A  G#  A
Become another casualty of soci - ety.
              E   B  C#m
I'll never fall in line,
                  G#     A      G#  A
Become another victim of your conformity,

And back (down.)
```

Link 1

‖ E | E A E | E A E | E A E | E A ‖

down.

Verse 2

N.C.   E   B
Because you don't know us at all, we laugh when old people fall,

     A
But what would you expect with a conscience so small?

         E   B
Heavy metal and mullets is how we were raised,

 A
Maiden and Priest were the gods that we praised.

        E
'Cause we like having fun at other people's expense and,

C♯m   A
Driving people down is just a minor offence then.

      E
It's none of your concern, I guess I'll never learn,

    C♯m   A
I'm sick of being told to wait my turn.

Chorus 2

             E   B   C♯m
I don't wanna waste my time,

           G♯   A   G♯   A
Become another casualty of soci - ety.

         E   B   C♯m
I'll never fall in line,

           G♯   A   G♯   A
Become another victim of your conformity,

And back (down.)

Link 2

| E | E | E | A | E | E | E | E | ‖

down.

Bridge

E   B/D♯   C♯m   A
Don't count on me, to let you know when.

E   B/D♯   C♯m   A
Don't count on me, I'll do it again.

E   B   C♯m   A
Don't count on me, it's the point you're missing,

E   B   C♯m   A
Don't count on me, 'cause I'm not listening.

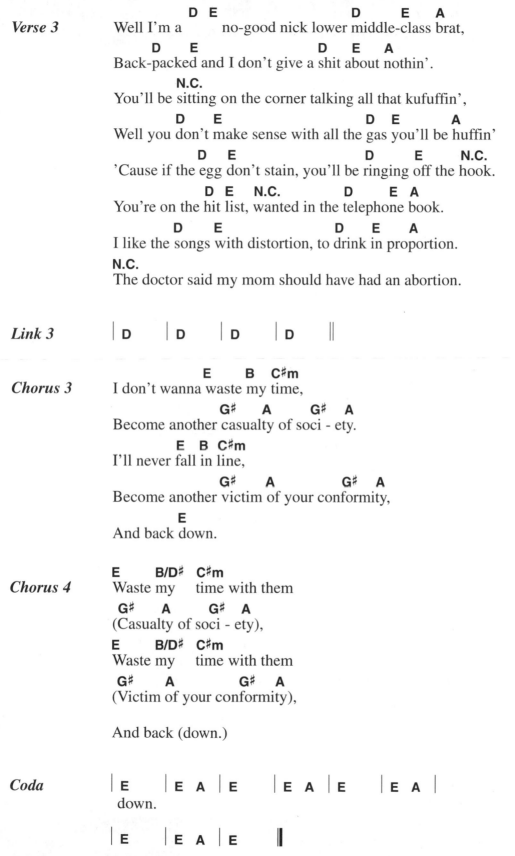

Verse 3

         D E   **D E A**
Well I'm a   no-good nick lower middle-class brat,
     D E   **D E A**
Back-packed and I don't give a shit about nothin'.
      N.C.
You'll be sitting on the corner talking all that kufuffin',
      D E   **D E   A**
Well you don't make sense with all the gas you'll be huffin'
       D E   **D E N.C.**
'Cause if the egg don't stain, you'll be ringing off the hook.
        D E N.C.   **D E A**
You're on the hit list, wanted in the telephone book.
       D E   **D E A**
I like the songs with distortion, to drink in proportion.
N.C.
The doctor said my mom should have had an abortion.

Link 3 | **D** | **D** | **D** | **D** ||

Chorus 3

         E   **B C♯m**
I don't wanna waste my time,
           G♯   **A**   **G♯** **A**
Become another casualty of soci - ety.
        E **B C♯m**
I'll never fall in line,
          G♯   **A**   **G♯** **A**
Become another victim of your conformity,
        E
And back down.

Chorus 4

 E   **B/D♯** **C♯m**
Waste my   time with them
 G♯   **A**   **G♯** **A**
(Casualty of soci - ety),
 E   **B/D♯** **C♯m**
Waste my   time with them
 G♯   **A**   **G♯** **A**
(Victim of your conformity),

And back (down.)

Coda | **E** | **E A** | **E** | **E A** | **E** | **E A** |
        down.

    | **E** | **E A** | **E**   ‖

F.E.A.R.

WORDS & MUSIC BY IAN BROWN, DAVE MCCRACKEN & DAVE COLQUHOUN

F#m7   A   D   Bm

Intro   ‖: F#m7 | A | D | Bm :‖ *Play 3 times*

Verse 1

       F#m7
For each a road,

            A
For every man a religion.

D   Bm
  Find everybody and rule

F#m7   A
  Everything and rumble.

D   Bm
  Forget everything and remember.

            F#m7
For everything a reason.

A   D   Bm
  Forgive everybody and remember.

Verse 2

       F#m7
For each a road,

            A
For every man a religion.

D   Bm
  Face everybody and rule

F#m7   A
  Everything and rumble.

D   Bm
  Forget everything and remember.

For everything a (reason.)

Link 1 | F#m7 | A | D | Bm ‖
  reason.

Chorus 1

F#m7   A
F. E. A. R.,   F. E. A. R.,

D   Bm
F. E. A. R.,   F. E. A. R..

Verse 3

F#m7
Finding eternity arouses reactions.

A
    Freeing excellence affects reality.

D
Fallen empires are running.

Bm
Find earth and reap.

Link 2

| F#m7 | A   ‖

Verse 4

      D   Bm
Fantastic expectations, amazing revelations.

F#m7
Final execution and resurrection.

A
    Free expression as revolution.

D   Bm
Finding everything and realising

Chorus 2

                F#m7   A
You got the fear, you got the fear,

                D   Bm
You got the fear, you got the fear.

{ ‖:   F#m7   A
    You got the fear,   you got the fear,
           F. E. A. R.   F. E. A. R.

{   D   Bm
    You got the fear,   you got the fear. :‖ *Play 3 times*
           F. E. A. R.   F. E. A. R.

Coda

                F#m7 A   D Bm
‖: You got the fear,   you got the fear.   :‖

‖: F#m7 | A | D | Bm :‖ *Repeat and fade*

FEEL GOOD HIT OF THE SUMMER

WORDS & MUSIC BY JOSHUA HOMME & NICK OLIVERI

B♭5   D♭5   E♭5
fr4   fr6

Intro   ‖: (B♭5) | (B♭5) | (B♭5) | (B♭5) :‖

Chorus 1

B♭5
Nicotine, Valium, Vicodin, Marijuana, Ecstasy and Alcohol, __

Nicotine, Valium, Vicodin, Marijuana, Ecstasy and Alcohol, __

Nicotine, Valium, Vicodin, Marijuana, Ecstasy and Alcohol, __

                                                                 D♭5
Nicotine, Valium, Vicodin, Marijuana, Ecstasy and Alcohol. ____

B♭5   D♭5
C-C-C-C-C-Co-caine.

Verse 1 | B♭5 | B♭5 | B♭5 | E♭5 |
                           C-C-C-C-C-Co-caine.

               | B♭5 | B♭5 | B♭5 | E♭5 |
                           Co - Co - caine.

               | B♭5 | B♭5 | B♭5 | E♭5 ‖
                           C-C-C-C-C-Co-caine.

Link | (B♭5) | (B♭5) | (B♭5) | (B♭5) ‖

Guitar solo | D♭5 | D♭5 | D♭5 | D♭5 |

                   | (B♭5) | (B♭5) | (B♭5) | (B♭5) ‖

Chorus 2   **B♭5**
Nicotine, Valium, Vicodin, Marijuana, Ecstasy and Alcohol, ___

Nicotine, Valium, Vicodin, Marijuana, Ecstasy and Alcohol, ___

Nicotine, Valium, Vicodin, Marijuana, Ecstasy and Alcohol, ___

Nicotine, Valium, Vicodin, Marijuana, Ecstasy and Alcohol, ___

Nicotine, Valium, Vicodin, Marijuana, Ecstasy and Alcohol, ___

                                                                 D♭5
Nicotine, Valium, Vicodin, Marijuana, Ecstasy and Alcohol. _____
B♭5   **D♭5**
C-C-C-C-C-Co-caine.

Verse 2 | **B♭5** | **B♭5** | **B♭5** | **E♭5** |
                                    C-C-C-C-C-Co-caine.

         | **B♭** | **B♭5** | **B♭5** | **D♭5**   ‖
                                  Co - Co - caine.

Chorus 2   **B♭5**
Nicotine, Valium, Vicodin, Marijuana, Ecstasy and Alcohol, ___

Nicotine, Valium, Vicodin, Marijuana, Ecstasy and Alcohol, ___

Nicotine, Valium, Vicodin, Marijuana, Ecstasy and Alcohol, ___

Nicotine, Valium, Vicodin, Marijuana, Ecstasy and Alcohol, ___

Nicotine, Valium, Vicodin, Marijuana, Ecstasy and Alcohol, ___

                                                       D♭5
Nicotine, Valium, Vicodin, Marijuana, C-C-C-C-C-Co-caine.

FEELING GOOD

WORDS & MUSIC BY LESLIE BRICUSSE & ANTHONY NEWLEY

B7add13   Em   Em7   Cmaj7   Em/B   B7sus4

B7   Em/C#   Em/A   Em/G   Em/F#   A7

C/E   Em6   G   Am7   F#7   D   C7

Capo third fret

Intro
| B7add13 | Em | Em |

Verse 1

Em   Em7 Cmaj7   Em/B
Birds flying high,   you know how I feel.

Em   Em7 Cmaj7   B7sus4 B7
Sun in the sky,   you know how I feel.

Em Em7   Em/C#   Cmaj7
Reeds drifting on by,   you know how I feel.

Chorus 1

Em/B   Em/A
It's a new dawn, it's a new day,

Em/G   Em/F#   A7 B7 N.C.
It's a new life for   me   and I'm feeling (good.)

Link 1
| Em   Em7 | Cmaj7   B7 |

good.

Verse 2

Em   Em7 Cmaj7   Em/B
Fish in the sea, you know how I feel.

Em   Em7 Cmaj7   B7sus4 B7
River running   free, you know how I feel.

Em   Em7 Em/C#   Cmaj7
Blossom in the trees,   you know how I feel.

Chorus 2

        Em/B   **Em/A**
It's a new dawn, it's a new day,

        Em/G   **Em/F♯** **A⁷** **B⁷** **N.C.**
It's a new life for   me   and I'm feeling good.

Link 2 | **Em**   **C/E** | **Em⁶**   **C/E** ‖

Verse 3

   (Em)   **(Em⁷)**
   Dragonfly out in the sun

 (Cmaj⁷)   **(Em/B)**   **(Em)**
   You know what I mean, don't you know.

         (Em⁷)
Butterflies all are having fun,

 (Cmaj⁷)   **(B⁷)**
   You know what I mean.

 (G)   **(Em)** **(Cmaj⁷)**   **(Am⁷)**
Sleep in peace   when day is done

         (G)   **(Em)**
And this old world is a new world

       (Cmaj⁷)   **(B⁷)**
And a bold world   for (me.)

Link 3 | **Em**   **Em⁷** | **Cmaj⁷** **Em/B** ‖
           me. _____

Verse 4

 Em   **Em⁷** **Cmaj⁷**   **Em/B**
   Stars when you shine, you know how I feel.

 Em   **Em⁷** **Cmaj⁷**   **B⁷sus⁴** **B⁷**
   Scent of the pine, you know how I feel.

      Em   **Em⁷** **Em/C♯**   **Cmaj⁷**
Yeah, freedom is mine and you know how I feel.

Chorus 3

       Em/B   **Em/A**
It's a new dawn, it's a new day,

       Em/G   **Em/F♯** **A⁷**
It's a new life for   me.

Link 4 | **F♯⁷** | **D** | **C⁷** | **B⁷** | **B⁷** **N.C.** ‖
           With scat vocals

Coda | **Em**   **Em⁷** | **Cmaj⁷** **Em/B** | **Em**   **Em⁷** | **Cmaj⁷** **Em/B** |

            | **Em**   **Em⁷** | **Em/C♯** **Cmaj⁷** | **Em/B** **Em/A** | **Em/G**   **Em/F♯** |
            A⁷ **B⁷** **N.C.**   **(Em)**
                Feeling good.

FOUND THAT SOUL

WORDS & MUSIC BY JAMES DEAN BRADFIELD, NICK JONES & SEAN MOORE

E   C#5   B   F#   A   G#5   C#m

Intro | E | C#5 | C#5 E | C#5 | C#5 E | C#5 | C#5 E ||

Verse 1

C#5   E
   Show me a wonder

C#5   E
   We can't be sure of,

C#5   E
   I exist in a place

C#5
   A self-made vacuum.

B   F#
   But I'm still stranded here

B   E
   With all the scum,

C#5   E
   So clean, so lost,

C#5
   So beautiful.

Chorus 1

A   G#5   C#m
But I found that soul,

         A
Yeah, I found that home

G#5   C#m | C#m   E |
But I found that soul.

A   G#5   C#m
But I found that soul,

         A
Yeah, I found that now

G#5   C#m | C#m E ||
But I found that soul.

Verse 2

C#5   E
Not a subject,
C#5   E
Not a subject am I,
C#5   E
Sick and pale but
C#5   E
Strangely alive.

B   F#
Broken blood-vessels
B   E
Line my cheeks,
C#5   E
Reflections look bad,
C#5
Somehow I'm real.

Chorus 2

A   G#5   C#m
But I found that soul,
                  A
Yeah, I found that home
G#5   C#m | C#m   E |
But I found that soul.
A   G#5   C#m
But I found that soul,
                  A
Yeah, I found that now
G#5   C#m | C#m   E ‖
But I found that soul.

Solo   ‖: A | G#5 | C#5 | C#5   :‖ *Play 4 times*

Chorus 3   As Chorus 2

Coda

C#5   ·   E
Show me a wonder,
C#5   E
Show me a wonder,
C#5   E
Show me a wonder,
C#5   E | C#m   ‖
Show me a wonder.

FLAVOR OF THE WEAK

WORDS & MUSIC BY STACY JONES

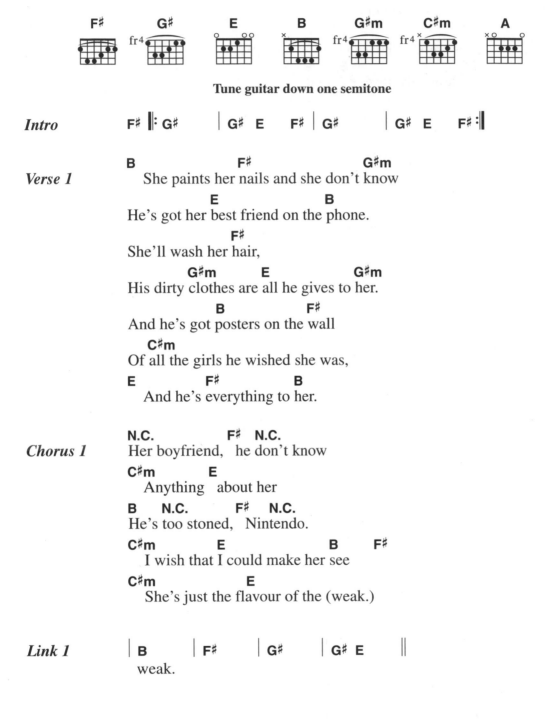

Tune guitar down one semitone

Intro F# ‖: G# | G# E F# | G# | G# E F# :‖

Verse 1

     B   **F#**   **G#m**
She paints her nails and she don't know
                    E   **B**
He's got her best friend on the phone.
             F#
She'll wash her hair,
          G#m   **E**   **G#m**
His dirty clothes are all he gives to her.
                B   **F#**
And he's got posters on the wall
     C#m
Of all the girls he wished she was,
E   **F#**   **B**
     And he's everything to her.

Chorus 1

N.C.   **F#** **N.C.**
Her boyfriend, he don't know
C#m   **E**
   Anything   about her
B **N.C.**   **F#** **N.C.**
He's too stoned, Nintendo.
C#m   **E**   **B**   **F#**
  I wish that I could make her see
C#m   **E**
  She's just the flavour of the (weak.)

Link 1 | B | F# | G# | G# E ‖
weak.

Verse 2

```
        B              F#                    G#m
            It's Friday night and she's all alone,
                E              B
        He's a million miles away.
                        F#               G#m
        She's dressed to kill but the TV's on:
                    E          G#m
        He's connected to the sound.
                        B               F#
        And he's got pictures on the wall
            C#m
        Of all the girls he's loved before
        E                  F#             B
            And she knows all his favourite songs.
```

Chorus 2

```
        N.C.            F#  N.C.
        Her boyfriend,   he don't know
        C#m         E
            Anything   about her
        B    N.C.       F#   N.C.
        He's too stoned,   Nintendo.
        C#m             E                 B     F#
            I wish that I could make her see
        C#m                   E
            She's just the flavour of the (weak.)
```

Link 2

```
        | B        | F#        ||
        weak.         Yeah!
```

Solo

```
        | G#        | G# E  F# | G#          | G# E  F# |

        | G#        | G# E  F# | G#          | G# E     ||

        | B      .  | F#        | C#m       | E         |

        | B         | F#        | C#m       | E       | E       ||
```

Chorus 3

       B
    Her boyfriend, he don't know

Anything about her.
           F♯
He's too stoned, he's too stoned,
C♯m   E
    He's too stoned, he's too stoned.

Chorus 4

B   F♯
Her boyfriend, he don't know
C♯m   E
    Anything   about her
B   F♯
He's too stoned, Nintendo.
C♯m   E   B   F♯
    I wish that I could make her see
C♯m   E   B   F♯
    She's just the flavour of the weak.

Coda

C♯m   E   B   F♯
    Yeah, she's the flavour of the weak,
C♯m   A
    She makes me weak.

JUST A DAY

WORDS & MUSIC BY GRANT NICHOLAS

A   E   C#m   G#   B   F#

Intro | (A) | (A) | (E) | (E) ||: A | A | E | E :||

Verse 1

    A   E
     Waking up at twelve in my clothes again,

                       A
Feel my head explode from a night of gin;

           E
Another night out   late.

   A   E
    I don't wanna drink, don't wanna be a clown,

                  A
Gotta get my feet back on the ground

           E
Before it pulls me   in.

Pre-chorus 1

  C#m   A   E
     How come it ended up like this?

  C#m   G#   A
     And who's gonna catch me when I'm coming down

           E
To hit the ground again?

Chorus 1

     B   A
All by myself

  C#m   E
    'Cause I don't wanna drag you down,

  B   A   E
Hold you down,   'cause you're a friend.

   B   A
I blame myself.

  C#m   F#   A
    I guess you think it's funny now, funny now.

Link ||: A | A | E | E :||

Verse 2

    N.C. **A**   **E**
On the underground with the freaks and frowns,

                         A
Looking at the world through silver clouds

          E
But then it all came down.

A   **E**
  I gotta rise above the emotional flood,

                   A
Gotta cut these ropes around my hands;

         E
Pull myself around.

Pre-chorus 2

C♯m   **A**   **E**
  How come it ended up like this?

C♯m   **G♯**   **A**
  And who's gonna be there when I've lost control?

              E
I'm heading to crash-land.

Chorus 2

    B   **A**
All by myself

C♯m   **E**
  'Cause I don't wanna drag you down,

B   **A**   **E**
Hold you down, 'cause you're a friend.

  B   **A**
I blame myself.

C♯m   **F♯**   **A**
  I guess you think it's funny now, funny now.

Solo   ‖: B C♯m | G♯ A | C♯m B | G♯ A :‖

Chorus 3

  E   **B**   **A**
  All by myself

C♯m   **E**
  'Cause I don't wanna drag you down,

B   **A**   **E**
Hold you down, 'cause you're a friend.

  B   **A**
I blame myself.

C♯m   **F♯**   **A**
  I guess you think it's funny now, funny now.

          E
It's such a shame.

Chorus 4

       B   **A**
All by myself

  C♯m   **E**
  'Cause I don't wanna drag you down,

B   **A**   **E**
Hold you down,   'cause you're a friend.

  B   **A**
I blame myself.

C♯m   **F♯**   **A**
  I guess you think it's funny now, funny now.

                E
It's such a sin.

Chorus 5

       B   **A**
All by myself

  C♯m   **E**
  'Cause I don't wanna drag you down,

B   **A**   **E**
Hold you down,   'cause you're a friend.

  B   **A**
I blame myself.

C♯m   **F♯**   **A**
  I guess you think it's funny now, funny now.

             Play 7 times

Coda   ‖: Do do-do do. :‖ **A**   ‖

GETTING AWAY WITH IT (ALL MESSED UP)

WORDS & MUSIC BY TIM BOOTH, JIM GLENNIE, SAUL DAVIES, MARK HUNTER & DAVID BAYNTON-POWER

Dm   F   C   G

Intro ‖: Dm | Dm | F | F | C | C | G | G :‖

Verse 1

Dm   F
  Are you aching for the blade?
       C   G
That's okay, we're insured.
Dm   F
  Are you aching for the grave?
       C   G
That's okay, we're insured.

Chorus 1

Dm   F
  We're getting away with it all messed up,
                 C   G
Getting away with it all messed up, that's the living.

Verse 2

Dm   F
  Daniel's saving Grace:
          C   G
She's out in deep water, hope he's a good swimmer.
Dm   F
  Daniel plays his ace
          C   G
Deep inside his temple: he knows how to surf her.

Chorus 2

Dm   F
 We're getting away with it all messed up,

         C   G
Getting away with it all messed up, that's the living.

Dm   F
 We're getting away with it all messed up,

         C   G
Getting away with it all messed up, that's the living.

Solo 1 | Dm | Dm | F | F | C | C | G | G ||

Verse 3

Dm   F
 Daniel drinks his weight,

         C   G
Drinks like Richard Burton, dance like John Travolta, now.

Dm   F
 Daniel's saving Grace,

         C   G
He was all but drowning, now they live like dolphins.

Chorus 3

Dm   F
 We're getting away with it all messed up,

         C   G
Getting away with it all messed up, that's the living.

Dm   F
 We're getting away with it all messed up,

         C   G
Getting away with it all messed up, that's the living.

Solo 2 | Dm | Dm | F | F | C | C | G | G ||

Chorus 4

Dm   F
 We're getting away with it (all messed up),

         C   G
Getting away with it (all messed up), that's the living.

 Dm   F
‖: Are we getting away with it (all messed up),

         C   G
Getting away with it (all messed up), that's the living. :‖

        Dm
That's the living.

HAVE A NICE DAY

WORDS & MUSIC BY KELLY JONES

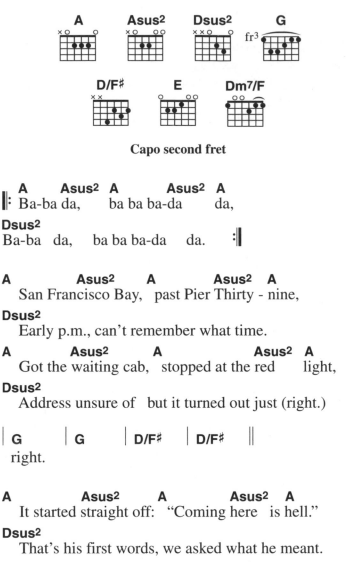

Capo second fret

Intro

    A   **Asus²** **A**   **Asus²** **A**

‖: Ba-ba da,   ba ba ba-da   da,

Dsus²

Ba-ba da,   ba ba ba-da   da.   :‖

Verse 1

A   **Asus²**   **A**   **Asus²** **A**

San Francisco Bay,   past Pier Thirty - nine,

Dsus²

Early p.m., can't remember what time.

A   **Asus²**   **A**   **Asus²** **A**

Got the waiting cab,   stopped at the red   light,

Dsus²

Address unsure of   but it turned out just (right.)

| **G** | **G** | **D/F♯** | **D/F♯** | ‖

right.

Verse 2

A   **Asus²**   **A**   **Asus²** **A**

It started straight off: "Coming here   is hell."

Dsus²

That's his first words, we asked what he meant.

A   **Asus²**   **A**   **Asus²** **A**

He said, "Where ya from?" We told him our   lot.

Dsus²

"When ya take a holiday is this what you (want?")

| **G** | **G** | **D/F♯** | **D/F♯** | ‖

want?"

Chorus 1

                    A
So have a ni - - - ce day, _____

            Dsus²
Have a ni - - - ce day, _____

                    A
Have a ni - - - ce day, _____

            Dsus²
Have a ni - - - ce day. _____

Verse 3

A   **Asus²**   **A**   **Asus²** **A**
   Lie around all day,   have a drink, a chase.
Dsus²
   Yourself and tourists, yeah, that's what I hate.

A   **Asus²**   **A**   **Asus²**   **A**
   He said, "We're going wrong,   we've all become the same:
Dsus²
   We dress the same ways, only our accents (change.")

| **G** | **G** | **D/F♯** | **D/F♯** ||
 change."

Chorus 2   As Chorus 1

Solo | **E** | **E** | **Dsus²** | **Dsus²** |

            | **E** | **E** | **Dsus²** | **Dm⁷/F** ||

            ‖: **A**   **Asus²** **A**   **Asus²** **A**
              Ba-ba da,   ba ba ba-da   da,
            Dsus²
            Ba-ba   da, ba ba ba-da da.   :‖

Verse 4

A   **Asus²** **A**   **Asus²** **A**
   Swim in the ocean,   that be my   dish:
Dsus²
   I drive around all day and kill processed fish.

A   **Asus²**   **A**   **Asus²** **A**
   It's all money-gum,   no artists any - more;
Dsus²
   You're only in it now to make more, more, (more.)

| **G** | **G** | **D/F♯** | **D/F♯** ||
 more.

Chorus 2   ‖: As Chorus 1 :‖   *Repeat to fade*

49

LAST RESORT

WORDS & MUSIC BY PAPA ROACH

E5   D5   C5   B5   D   G5

Intro

N.C.
Cut my life into pieces,

This is my last resort.

E5   D5
  Suffocation,   no breathing,

C5   B5   D5 | E5   D5 |
Don't give a fuck if I cut my arm bleeding.

C5   B5   D5
  This is my last resort.

| E5   D5 | C5   B5 D5 ||

Verse 1

E5   D5
  Cut my life into pieces,

      C5
I've reached my last resort.

     B5   D5
Suffocation, no breathing,

E5   D5
Don't give a fuck if I cut my arm bleeding.

C5   B5   D5
  Do you even care if I die bleeding?

Verse 2

E5   D5
  Would it be wrong, would it be right,

     C5
If I took my life tonight?

B5   D5
Chances are that I might,

E5   D5
  Mutilation out of sight,

        C5   B5   D5
And I'm contemplating suicide.

Chorus 1

       E5   **C5**
'Cause I'm losing my sight, losing my mind,

D
Wish somebody would tell me I'm fine.

E5   **C5**
Losing my sight, losing my mind,

D
Wish somebody would tell me I'm fine.

Link | **E5** **D5** | **C5** **B5** **D5** ||

Verse 3

  E5   **D5**
  I never realised I was spread too thin

   C5   **B5**   **D5**
'Til it was too late and I was empty within.

     E5   **D5**
Hungry, feeding on chaos and living in sin,

C5   **B5** **D5**
Downward spiral, where do I begin?

E5   **D5**
 It all started when I lost my mother,

   C5   **B5**   **D5**
No love for myself and no love for another.

      E5   **D5**
Searching to find a love upon a higher level,

     C5   **B5**   **D5**
Finding nothing but questions and devils.

Chorus 2 As Chorus 1

Bridge 1

E5   **C5** **G5**   **B5**
Nothing's alright, nothing is fine.

E5 **C5**   **G5** **B5**
 I'm running and I'm cry - ing.

E5 **G5**   **C5** **B5** **E5**   **G5**   **C5**   **B5**
 I'm crying, __ I'm crying, __ I'm crying, __ I'm crying.

E5 **D5**   **C5** **B5** **D5**
 I can't go on

E5   **D5** **C5** **B5** **D5**
 Liv - ing this   way.

Verse 4

E5   D5
  Cut my life into pieces,

C5
  This is my last resort.

E5   D5
  Suffocation, no breathing,

C5   Bm
Don't give a fuck if I cut my arm bleeding.

Verse 5

E5   D5
  Would it be wrong, would it be right,

    C5
If I took my life tonight?

B5   D5
Chances are that I might,

E5   D5
  Mutilation out of sight,

         C5   B5   D5
And I'm contemplating suicide.

Chorus 3

           E5   C5
'Cause I'm losing my sight, losing my mind,

D
Wish somebody would tell me I'm fine.

E5   C5
Losing my sight, losing my mind,

D
Wish somebody would tell me I'm fine.

Bridge 2

E5   C5 G5   B5
Nothing's alright, nothing is fine.

E5   C5   G5 B5
  I'm running and I'm cry - ing.

Coda

E5 C5   D5   E5 C5 D5
I   can't go on liv - ing this way,

| E5   C5   D5 | E5   C5 D5 | |
                                   Can't go on, ___

| E5   C5 D | | E5   C5 |
        Living this way

| D5 | E5 | E5   ‖
Nothing's all   right!

A LITTLE RESPECT

WORDS & MUSIC BY VINCE CLARKE & ANDY BELL

C   Csus⁴   G   Gsus⁴   E

Esus⁴   F   Asus²   Am   Em   G/B

Intro | C Csus⁴ | C Csus⁴ | C Csus⁴ | C   ‖

Verse 1
                   C   Csus⁴
I tried to discover _____

C   Csus⁴   G   Gsus⁴ G
  A little something to make me sweeter,

    Gsus⁴ E   Esus⁴ E   Esus⁴   F
Oh baby, refrain _____   from breaking my heart.

N.C.   C   Csus⁴
I'm so in love with you,

C   Csus⁴ G   Gsus⁴ G
  I'll be   forever blue

Gsus⁴   F
That you give me no reason,

                                 Asus² Am
You know you're making me work so hard.

G
That you give me no, that you give me no,

That you give me no, that you give me no

Chorus 1
C   Csus⁴ C   Csus⁴ Asus² Am
Soul, _____ I hear you call - ing.

Asus² Am F
    Oh baby please (give a little respect to me),

                 Em F   G
Give a little respect to ____ (me.)

| C Csus⁴ | C Csus⁴ | C Csus⁴ | C   ‖
me. _____

Verse 2

                      C   Csus4
And if I should falter,

C   Csus4   G   Gsus4   G
Would you open your arms out to me?

          Gsus4   E   Esus4
We can make love not war,

E   Esus4   F
And live with peace in our hearts.

     G Asus2 G/B C   Csus4
I'm   so   in love with you,

C   Csus4 G Gsus4
 I'll be   forever blue.

G   Gsus4   F
What religion or reason

                         Asus2 Am
Could drive a man to forsake his lover?

G
Don't you tell me no, don't you tell me no,

                      F   G
Don't you tell me no, don't you tell me no

Chorus 2

C   Csus4 C   Csus4 Asus2 Am
Soul, ________ I hear you call - ing.

Asus2 Am F
   Oh baby please (give a little respect to me),

           Em   F G
Give a little respect to ___ (me.)

| C Csus4 | C Csus4 | C Csus4 | C | ‖
me. ___________________

Guitar solo | B♭ | B♭ | G   ‖

Verse 3

G   C   Csus4
  I'm so in love with you,

C   Csus4 G   Gsus4
 I'll be   forever blue

G Gsus4   F
  That you give me no reason,

                     Asus2 Am
You know you're making me work so hard

G
That you give me no, that you give me no,

                   F   G
That you give me no, that you give me no

Chorus 3

C   Csus⁴   C   Csus⁴   Asus²   Am
Soul, _____ I hear you call - ing.

Asus²   Am   F
Oh baby please (give a little respect to me),

                   Em   F   G   C   Csus⁴
Give a little respect to ___ me.

Coda

C   Csus⁴   Asus²   Am
I hear you call - ing.

Asus²   Am   F
Oh baby please (give a little respect to me),

                   Em   F   G
Give a little respect to ___

| **C Csus⁴** | **C Csus⁴** | **C Csus⁴** | **C** |

me. _____

LET IT LIVE

WORDS & MUSIC BY GARY BRIGGS, NATHAN WASON & IWAN GRONOW

Chord diagrams: B5, Bm, Bsus4 (fr2), G, A, D

Dsus2/C♯, Gmaj7, B♭maj7, C, Dsus2, Bsus2

Tune guitar slightly sharp

Intro
| B5 | B5 | B5 | B5 | B5 | B5 ||

Verse 1
      Bm   Bsus4
Can you be part of something, without thought for self or mind?
           G   Bm
You're still soul-searching for the right line.

Verse 2
Bm   Bsus4
Need no excuse to wander, 'cause it's more than you can take.
        G   Bm G
You stay true, no-one's gonna pull you out.

Chorus 1
A   D   Dsus2/C♯ Bm
Let it live, _____
        D   Dsus2/C♯ Bm
Let it live, _____
        D   A Bm
Let it breathe _____
         A   G Gmaj7 A
Life today. _____

Link 1
| B5 | B5 ||

Verse 3
      B5   Bsus4
Can you be part of something, even though you're still unsure?
        G   Bm G
You stay true but no-one's gonna pull you out.

Chorus 2

```
        A    D      Dsus2/C♯  Bm
Let it live, _____
             D      Dsus2/C♯  Bm
Let it live, _____
             D    A    Bm
Let it breathe _____
                A      G
Life today. _____
```

Chorus 3

```
        A    D      Dsus2/C♯  Bm
Let it live, _____
             D      Dsus2/C♯  Bm
Let it live, _____
             D    A    Bm
Let it breathe _____
             B♭maj7  C   Dsus2
Life today, _____
             B♭maj7   C
Life to - day. _____
```

Link 2

```
| Bm   | N.C.   | N.C.   | N.C.   ||
```

Instrumental

```
| Bm  Bsus2 | Bm  Bsus2 | Bm  Bsus2 | G   A   ||
                                          Let it
```

Chorus 4

```
D      Dsus2/C♯  Bm
Live, _____
       D      Dsus2/C♯  Bm
Let it live, _____
       D    A    Bm
Let it breathe _____
          A       G  Gmaj7
Life today. _____
```

Chorus 5

```
       D      Dsus2/C♯  Bm
Let it live, _____
       D      Dsus2/C♯  Bm
Let it live, _____
       D    A    Bm
Let it breathe _____
          B♭maj7  C   Dsus2
‖: Life today. _____   :‖   Play 4 times
```

MUSCLE MUSEUM

LYRICS & MUSIC BY MATTHEW BELLAMY

F#m   C#   F#   Bm   C#7/G#   D5   Dadd#11

E   C#/E#   F#m7   D   A   C#/G#   E7

Intro ‖: F#m | C# | F#m F# | Bm :‖

Verse 1
(F#m)   (C#)   (F#m)
She had something to confess to, but you don't have the time,
         (Bm)
So look the other way.
(F#m)   (C#)   (F#m)
You will wait until it's over to reveal what you'd never shown her,
         (Bm)
Too little much too   late.

Link 1 | F#m | C# | F#m | Bm ‖

Verse 2
F#m   C#
Too long trying to resist it,
                       F#m
You've just gone and missed it.
                       Bm
It's escaped your   world.

Link 2 | F#m | C#7/G# | D5 | Dadd#11 D5 ‖

Chorus 1
F#m   C#7/G#
Can you see that I am needing,
                       F#m   Bm
Begging for so much more than you could ever give?

cont.

        F♯m   C♯7/G♯
And I don't want you to adore me,

                    F♯m   Bm
Don't want you to ignore me when it pleases you.

      E   C♯7/G♯   (F♯m) | (F♯m)   ‖
Yeah, and I'll do it on my own.

Link 3 | F♯m | C♯ | F♯m F♯ | Bm   ‖

Verse 3

F♯m   C♯
I have played in every toilet

                F♯m
But you still want to spoil it

                Bm
To prove I've made a big mistake.

F♯m   C♯
Too long trying to resist it

                F♯m
You've just gone and missed it:

                Bm
It's escaped your world.

Link 4 | F♯m | C♯7/G♯ | D5 | Dadd♯11 D5 ‖

Chorus 2

F♯m   C♯7/G♯
Can you see that I am needing,

                F♯m   Bm
Begging for so much more than you could ever give?

      F♯m   C♯7/G♯
And I don't want you to adore me,

                F♯m   Bm
Don't want you to ignore me when it pleases you,

      E
Yeah. _____

Solo | C♯/E♯ | F♯m F♯m7 | D | E7 |

           | C♯/E♯ | F♯m F♯m7 | D | A   ‖

Coda | C♯/G♯ | F♯m Bm | F♯m Bm |

          | F♯m Bm | F♯m Bm | F♯m   ▐

NITE AND FOG

WORDS & MUSIC BY JONATHAN DONAHUE, GRASSHOPPER & JEFF MERCEL

Am   F/C   C   B♭   B♭/D   F   E♭   B♭6

fr3

Capo fourth fret

Intro | Am F/C | C | Am F/C | C   ‖

Verse 1

     Am F/C   C
If God moves across the water
       Am F/C   C
Then the girl moves in other ways,
       Am F/C   C
And I'm losing sight of either,
Am   F/C   C
Nite and fog are my days.

Verse 2

     Am   F/C   C
I wanted only to be gentle
       Am   F/C   C
But I gave her jealousy and rage.
       Am   F/C   C
Who knows exactly what I'm after?
Am   F/C   C
Nite and fog are my days.

Bridge 1

B♭   C   B♭/D   F
Wisemen want faith, fools want gold,
E♭   B♭6   F
Sailors want water but you want it (all.)

| Am F/C | C | Am F/C | C   ‖
all. _____

Verse 3

     Am   F   C
I tried to guide my love by starlite
       Am   F   C
And soon my life became a maze.

cont.

    Am   **F**   **C**
Osiris and Orion were your favourites;
Am   **F**   **C**
Nite and fog are my days.

Link

‖: **Am F/C** | **C** | **Am F/C** | **C**   :‖

Bridge 2

B♭   **C**   **B♭/D**   **F**
Vampires want darkness, monsters want souls,
E♭   **B♭6**   **F**
Spiders want corners but you want it (all.)

| **Am F/C** | **C** | **Am F/C** | **C**   ‖
all. _____

Verse 4

      Am   **F/C**   **C**
She turns half nude to find me naked
        Am   **F/C**   **C**
But I can see she wants me in other ways.
      Am   **F/C**   **C**
In the dark I've driven her to madness.
Am   **F/C**   **C**
Nite and fog are my days.

Verse 5

     Am   **F/C**   **C**
I hope you see your ship come in,
       Am   **F/C**   **C**
May it find you and never lose its way.
    Am   **F/C**   **C**
But I would make a poor captain.
Am   **F/C**   **C**
Nite and fog are my days.

Bridge 3

B♭   **C**   **B♭/D**   **F**
Vampires want darkness, monsters want souls,
E♭   **B♭6**   **F**
Spiders want corners but you want it (all.)

| **Am F/C** | **C**   ‖
all. _____

Coda

‖:   **Am**   **F/C**   **C**
But you _____ want it all.

| **Am F/C** | **C**   :‖ *Repeat to fade*

OCEAN SPRAY

WORDS BY JAMES DEAN BRADFIELD
MUSIC BY JAMES DEAN BRADFIELD, NICK JONES & SEAN MOORE

| Em | D | Am | Gsus2 |

| Bm7 | Am7 | A♭ (fr4) | Fm | Gmaj7 (fr5) |

Intro
| Em | Em D | Em | Em D ||

Verse 1

Em   Am
 It's easy to see, it's easy to see,

   D   Gsus2
To see only white, where colour should be.

Em   Am
 It's easy to feel, it's easy to feel,

   D   Gsus2
But it's not good enough even though it's real.

Chorus 1

Bm7   Am7
 Oh, please stay awake

   D   Gsus2
And then we can drink some ocean spray.

Bm7   Am7
 Oh please stay awake

   D   Gsus2
And then we can drink some ocean spray.

Link 1
| A♭ | Fm | Gsus2 | Gsus2 |

| A♭ | Fm | Gmaj7 | Gmaj7 ||

Verse 2

     Em   **Am**
It's easy to breathe, it's easy to breathe,
           D   **Gsus²**
To breathe only air where life should be.
Em   **Am**
It's easy to laugh, it's easy to cry,
          D   **Gsus²**
To cry so, so hard that it can't be denied.

Chorus 2   As Chorus 1

Link 2 | A♭ | Fm | Gsus² | Gsus² |

              | A♭ | Fm | Gmaj⁷ | Gmaj⁷ ||

Trumpet solo ‖: Em | Em | Am | Am |

                | D | D | Gsus² | Gsus² :‖

Chorus 3   As Chorus 1

Outro   ‖: A♭ | Fm | Gsus² | Gsus² :‖ *Play 3 times*

         | A♭ | Fm | Gsus² ‖

ONE STEP CLOSER

WORDS & MUSIC BY CHESTER BENNINGTON, ROB BOURDON, BRAD DELSON, JOSEPH HAHN & MIKE SHINODA

D5   E5   B♭5   A5   C5

fr5   fr7   fr6   fr5   fr3

G5   E♭sus2   F5   A♭5

fr3   fr6   fr4

Tune guitar down one semitone

Intro | D5 | D5 | D5 | D5 |

| D5 E5 B♭5 A5 C5 | D5 E5 B♭5 A5 C5 | D5 E5 B♭5 A5 C5 | D5 E5 B♭5 A5 C5 ||

     D5   E5 B♭5 A5 C5 D5 E5 B♭5 A5 C5

Verse 1   I cannot take this anymore, _____

     D5   E5   B♭5 A5 C5   D5   B♭5 A5 C5

     Saying everything I've said before. _____

     D5   E5   B♭5   A5 C5

All these words they make no sense,

     D5   E5   B♭5   A5 C5

I found bliss in ig - norance.

     D5   E5   B♭5 A5   C5

Less I hear the less you say,

     D5   E5   B♭5 A5   C5   G5

You'll find that out an - y - way, _____

Just like before.

     D5   C5   A5

Chorus 1   Everything you say to me _____

         B♭5   G5   A5

(Sends me one step closer to the edge

     E♭5   D5

And I'm about to break.)

         C5   A5

I need a little room to breathe _____

         B♭5   G5   A5

('Cause I'm one step closer to the edge

     E♭sus2   D5

I'm about to break.)

Verse 2

     E5   B♭5 A5 C5   D5 E5 B♭5 A5 C5
I find the ans - wers aren't so clear,

  D5   E5   B♭5 A5 C5 D5 E5 B♭5 A5 C5
  Wish I could find a way to disappear.

  D5   E5   B♭5 A5 C5
All these thoughts they make no sense,

  D5   E5 B♭5 A5 C5
I found bliss in ig - norance.

  D5   E5   B♭5 A5 C5
Nothing seems to go away,

  D5   E5 B♭5 A5 C5
Over and over again,

  G5
  Just like before.

Chorus 2

  As chorus 1

Chorus 2

  D5   C5   A5
  Everything you say to me _____

           B♭5   G5   A5
(Sends me one step closer to the edge

E♭sus2   D5
I'm about to break.)

            C5   A5
I need a little room to breathe _____

           B♭5   G5   A5
('Cause I'm one step closer to the edge

     E♭sus2
And I'm about to…)

Link

| D5 | D5 | D5 | D5 |
                                              Shut up when I'm talking to you!

‖: E♭5 D5 F5 A♭5 :‖ *Play 3 times*
  Shut up!

| E♭5   D5   E♭5 |
  Shut up when I'm talking to you!

‖: E♭5 D5 F5 A♭5 :‖ *Play 3 times*
  Shut up!

| E♭5 D5   ‖
Shut up _____ I'm about to (break.)

65

Chorus 3

$\{$

D5   C5 A5
 Everything you say to me _____
break.

   B♭5 G5   A5
(Sends me one step closer to the edge

 E♭5   D5
And I'm about to break.)

     C5 A5
I need a little room to breathe _____

    B♭5 G5   A5
('Cause I'm one step closer to the edge

  E♭sus2 D5
And I'm about to break.)

D5   C5 A5
 Everything you say to me _____

   B♭5 G5   A5
(Sends me one step closer to the edge

 E♭sus2 D5
And I'm about to break.)

     C5 A5
I need a little room to breathe _____

    B♭5 G5   A5
('Cause I'm one step closer to the edge

  E♭sus2
And I'm about to…)

Coda | E♭sus2 | N.C.   ‖
          Break!

SHINING LIGHT

WORDS & MUSIC BY TIM WHEELER

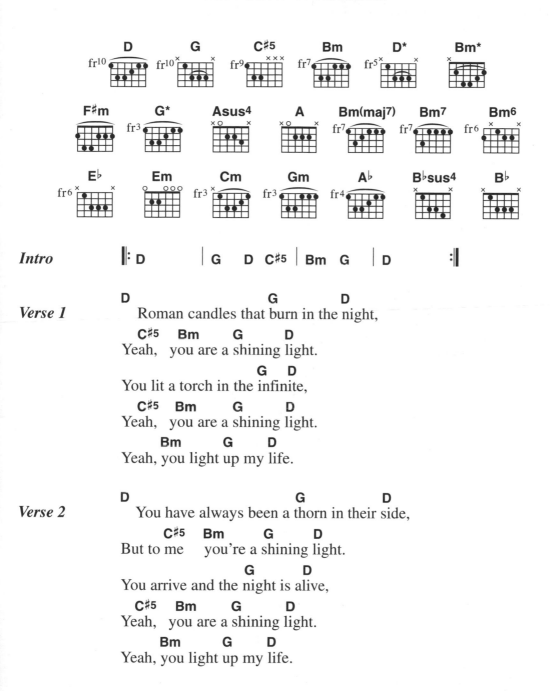

Intro ‖: D │ G D C#5 │ Bm G │ D :‖

Verse 1

    D   G   D

Roman candles that burn in the night,

  C#5 Bm   G   D

Yeah, you are a shining light.

                           G   D

You lit a torch in the infinite,

  C#5 Bm   G   D

Yeah, you are a shining light.

          Bm   G   D

Yeah, you light up my life.

Verse 2

    D   G   D

You have always been a thorn in their side,

     C#5 Bm   G   D

But to me   you're a shining light.

                           G   D

You arrive and the night is alive,

  C#5 Bm   G   D

Yeah, you are a shining light.

          Bm   G   D

Yeah, you light up my life.

Chorus 1

    D*   **Bm***
We made a connection,

  F♯m   **G***
A full on chemical reaction,

       F♯m   **G***
Brought by dark divine intervention,

     Asus4   **A**
Yeah, you are a shining light.

   D*   **Bm***   **F♯m**   **G***
A constellation once seen over Royal David's city,

   F♯m   **G***
An epiphany, you burn so pretty,

     Asus4   **A**
Yeah, you are a shining light.

Verse 3

  D   **G**   **D**
   You are a force, you are a constant source,

 C♯5 **Bm**   **G**   **D**
Yeah,   you are a shining light.

            G   **D**
Incandescent in the darkest night,

 C♯5 **Bm**   **G**   **D**
Yeah, you are a shining light.

  D   **G** **D**
   My mortal blood I would sacrifice,

 C♯5 **Bm**   **G**   **D**
For you are a shining light.

            G   **D**
Sov'reign bride of the infinite,

 C♯5 **Bm**   **G**   **D**
Yeah,   you are a shining light.

    Bm   **G**   **D**
Yeah, you light up my life.

Chorus 2   As Chorus 1

Bridge

Bm   **Bm(maj7)**
These are the days, you often say,

   Bm7   **Bm6**
There's nothing we cannot do.

 Em   **A**
Beneath a canopy of stars

 Em   **A**
I'd shed blood for you.

cont.

  Bm   **Bm(maj7)**
North star in the firmament,
      Bm7   **Bm6**
You shine the most bright.
        Em   **A**
I've seen you draped in an electric veil,
G*   **A**
Shrouded in celestial light.

Solo

‖: D* | Bm* | F♯m | G* | |

| F♯m | G* | Asus4 | A* :‖ Asus4 | A ‖

Chorus 3

E♭   **Cm**
We made a connection,
    Gm   **A♭**
A full on chemical reaction,
        Gm   **A♭**
Brought by dark divine intervention.
      B♭sus4   **B♭**
Yeah, you are a shining light,
     E♭   **Cm**   **Gm**   **A♭**
A constellation once seen over Royal David's city,
    Gm   **A♭**
An epiphany, you burn so pretty,
      B♭sus4   **B♭**
Yeah, you are a shining light.

Coda

      B♭sus4   **B♭**
Yeah, you light up my life,
      B♭sus4   **B♭**
Yeah, you are a shining light,
      B♭sus4   **B♭**   **E♭**
Yeah, you light up my life.

SING

WORDS & MUSIC BY FRAN HEALY

Em7 **Am7** **G** **D**

Capo second fret

Intro ‖: **Em7** | **Am7** | **Am7** | **Em7** :‖

Verse 1

Em7   **Am7**
Baby, you've been going so crazy,

                              Em7
Lately, nothing seems to be going right.

                              Am7
So low, why do you have to get so low?

                              Em7
You're so, you've been waiting in the sun too long.

Chorus 1

        G   **D**   **Am7**
But if you sing, sing,

              G
Sing, sing, sing, sing.

              D   **Am7**
For the love you bring won't mean a thing

                        G
Unless you sing, sing, sing, sing.

Verse 2

Em7   **Am7**
Colder, crying over your shoulder,

                              Em7
Hold her, tell her everything's gonna be fine.

                              Am7
Surely, you've been going too hurry,

                              Em7
Hurry, 'cause no one's gonna be stopped, now, now, now, now, now,

Chorus 2

       G   **D**   **Am⁷**
But if you sing, ____

           G
Sing, sing, sing, sing.

                   D   **Am⁷**
For the love you bring won't mean a thing

Unless you sing, sing, sing,
G
    Sing, sing, sing, sing.

Link   ‖: **G** **D** | **Am⁷** | **Am⁷** | **G**   :‖

Verse 3

Em⁷   **Am⁷**
Baby, there's something going on   today

           Em⁷
But I say   nothing, nothing, nothing,

                  Am⁷   **Em⁷**
Nothing, nothing,   nothing, nothing ...

Chorus 3

                                  G   **D**   **Am⁷**
Now, now, now, now, now, but if you sing, sing,

           G
Sing, sing, sing, sing.

                 D   **Am⁷**
For the love you bring won't mean a thing

                    G
Unless you sing, sing, sing, sing.

Chorus 3

        G   **D**   **Am⁷**
Oh baby sing, sing,

           G
Sing, sing, sing, sing.

                 D   **Am⁷**
For the love you bring won't mean a thing
           N.C.   **G**
Unless you sing, sing, sing, sing.

SLAVE TO THE WAGE

WORDS & MUSIC BY BRIAN MOLKO, STEFAN OLSDAL, STEVE HEWITT, STEPHEN MALKMUS & SCOTT KANNBERG

A   E   D   A7   Dmaj7   Amaj7

Capo first fret

Intro
| A | A | A | A | E | E |

| D | D | A | A | A | A |

Verse 1

A
    Run away from all your boredom,

Run away from all your whoredom,
    E   **D**
And wave your worries

And cares good - (bye.)

Link 1
| A | A | A | A |
  -bye.

Verse 2

A
    All it takes is one decision,

A lot of guts, a little vision,
    E   **D**
To wave your worries

And cares good - (bye.)

Link 2
| A | A | A |
  -bye.

Chorus 1

    A   **E**   **D**   **A**
    It's a maze for rats to try,
          E   **D**   **A⁷**
    It's a maze for rats to try,
          E   **D**   **A** | **A** | **A** |
    It's a race, a race for rats, a race for rats to die.
    A   **E**   **D**
    It's a race, a race for rats, a race for rats to (die.)

Link 3

  | **A** | **A** | **A** | **A**   ‖: **(A)** | **(A)** | **(A)** | **(A)**   :‖
  die.

Verse 3

    A
      Sick and tired of Maggie's farm,

    She's a bitch with broken arms
      E   **D**
    To wave your worries

    And cares good - (bye.)

Link 4

  | **A** | **A** | **A**   ‖
  -bye.

Chorus 2

    A   **E**   **D**   **A**
    It's a maze for rats to try,
          E   **D**   **A⁷**
    It's a maze for rats to try,
          E   **D**   **A** | **A** | **A** |
    It's a race, a race for rats, a race for rats to die.
    A   **E**   **Dmaj⁷**
    It's a race, a race for rats, a race for rats to (die.)

Link 5

  | **A** | **Amaj⁷** | **A** | **Amaj⁷** ‖: **(A)** | **(A)** | **(A)** | **(A)**   :‖
  die.

Chorus 3

        E   **Dmaj⁷**   **A** | **Amaj⁷** | **A** |
    It's a race, a race for rats, a race for rats to die.
    Amaj⁷ E   **Dmaj⁷**   **A**
    It's a race, a race for rats, a race for rats to die.

Coda

        Amaj⁷ A   **Amaj⁷ E**   **Dmaj⁷**   **A**
  ‖: Run away,   run away,   run away, run away. :‖
    A
    Run away.

SOULJACKER PART 1

WORDS & MUSIC BY E, BUTCH & ADAM SIEGEL

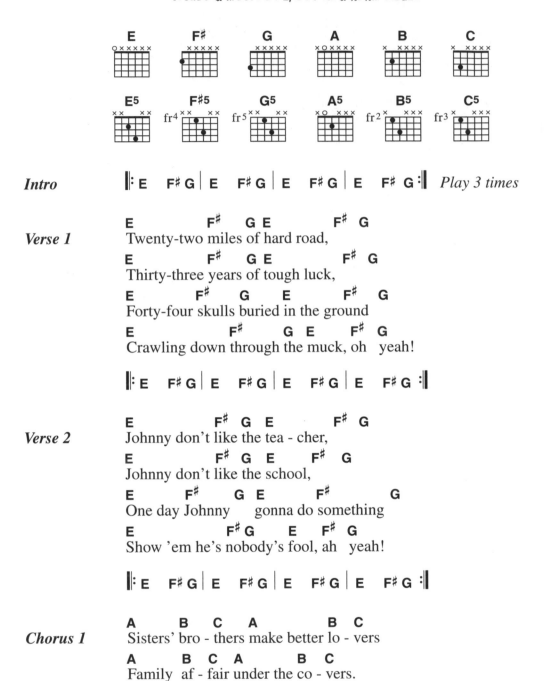

Intro ‖: E F♯ G E F♯ G │ E F♯ G │ E F♯ G :‖ *Play 3 times*

Verse 1
E   F♯ G E   F♯ G
Twenty-two miles of hard road,
E   F♯   G E   F♯ G
Thirty-three years of tough luck,
E   F♯   G E   F♯   G
Forty-four skulls buried in the ground
E   F♯   G E   F♯ G
Crawling down through the muck, oh yeah!

‖: E F♯ G │ E F♯ G │ E F♯ G │ E F♯ G :‖

Verse 2
E   F♯ G E   F♯ G
Johnny don't like the tea - cher,
E   F♯ G E   F♯   G
Johnny don't like the school,
E   F♯   G E   F♯   G
One day Johnny   gonna do something
E   F♯ G   E F♯ G
Show 'em he's nobody's fool, ah yeah!

‖: E F♯ G │ E F♯ G │ E F♯ G │ E F♯ G :‖

Chorus 1
A   B   C A   B C
Sisters' bro - thers make better lo - vers
A   B   C A   B C
Family af - fair under the co - vers.

cont.

E   F# G E   F#   G
Trailer park of   broken hearts,

         E   F#   G E   F#   G
Won't let you leave un - til you're bleeding.

‖: E F#G | E F#G | E F#G | E F#G :‖

Verse 3

E   F# G E   F# G
Sally don't like her daddy,

E   F#   G E   F# G
Sally don't like her friends,

E   F#   G E   F# G
Sally and Johnny   watching T. V.

E   F# G E F# G
Waiting for it to end, oh yeah!

‖: E F#G | E F#G | E F#G | E F#G :‖

Chorus 2

A   B   C   A   B   C
Sisters, bro - thers, make good lo - vers

A   B   C A   B C
Family-fare down under the co - vers.

E   F# G E   F#   G
Trailer in the park,   broken hearts,

         E   F# G E   F#   G
Won't let you leave un - til you… rock!

Guitar solo

‖: E5 F#5 G5 | E5 F#5 G5 | E5 F#5 G5 | E5 F#5 G5 :‖

| A5 B5 C5 | A5 B5 C5 | A5 B5 C5 | A5 B5 C5 |

| E5 F#5 G5 | E5 F#5 G5 | E5 F#5 G5 | E5 F#5 G5 |

‖: E5 | E5 | E5 | E5   :‖   *Play 11 times*

| E F#G | E F#G | E F#G | E F#G |

Verse 4

E   F#   GE   F# G
Twenty-two miles of hard road,

E   F   GE   F G
Thirty-three years of tough luck,

E   F#   G   E   F#   G
Forty-four skulls buried in the ground

E   F#   GE   F# G   E
Crawling down through the muck, oh yeah!

SUNRISE

WORDS & MUSIC BY JARVIS COCKER, NICK BANKS, CANDIDA DOYLE, STEPHEN MACKEY & MARK WEBBER

A   G/A   A*   D/A   G   G*   D   G/A*

Dm6/A   D*   A**   Dm   A7   Am7   D6/9/A   Am/E

Intro

| A | A G/A | A* | A* D/A |

| A* | A* G/A | A | A G ||

Verse 1

A
I used to hate the sun
           G*   A*
Because it shone on everything I'd done
          D   A*
And made me feel that all that I'd done
             G*   A   G
Was over-fill the ashtray of my life.
A   G*   A*
All my achievements in days of yore
           D   A*
Range from "pathetic" to "piss-poor",
   G*   A
But all that's gonna change.

Chorus 1

       A   G/A*   A
Because here comes sunrise,
        G/A*   A
Yeah, here's your sunrise.

Verse 2

       A
I used to hide from the sun,
  Dm6/A   A*
Tried to live my whole life underground.

　　　　　　　　　D/A　　　　　　　**A***
Oh, why'd you have to rise, and ruin all my fun?
　　　　　　　　　　　　G/A　　　**A**
Just turn over, close the curtains on the day.

Chorus 2
　　　　　　　G/A*　　**A**
But here comes sunrise,
　　　　　　　G/A* A
Yeah, here's your sunrise.

Bridge
　　　　　　　　　D*　　　　　　　　**A****
When you've been awake all night long
　　　　　Dm　　　　　　　　**A****
And you feel like crashing out at dawn,
　　　　　　Dm
But you've been awake all night

　　　　　　　　　　　　A**
So why should you crash out at dawn?

Coda　　‖: **A****　　| **A7**　　| **Am7**　　| **D6/9/A** :‖　*Play 8 times*

　　　　‖: **A****　　| **A7**　　| **Am/E**　　| **D*** :‖　*Play 4 times*

　　　　‖: **A****　　| **A7**　　| **Am7**　　| **D6/9/A** :‖　*Play 8 times*

　　　　‖: **A****　　| **A7**　　| **Am/E**　　| **D*** :‖　*Play 4 times*

　　　　‖: **A****　　| **A7**　　| **Am7**　　| **D6/9/A** :‖　*Play 4 times*

STACKED ACTORS

WORDS & MUSIC BY DAVE GROHL, TAYLOR HAWKINS & NATE MENDEL

Chord diagrams: A G F D Am7 A13 A7♭5 (fr4) E♭ (fr6)

Intro
‖: (A) | (G) | (F) | (D) :‖‖ A | G | F | D :‖

‖: Am7 A13 | Am7 A13 | Am7 A13 | Am7 A13 A7♭5 A13 :‖

Verse 1

Am7   A13   Am7   A13
Oh mirror mirror, you're coming in clear,

Am7   A13   Am7 A13 A7♭5 A13
I'm finally somewhere in between.

Am7   A13   Am7   A13
I'm impressed,what a beautiful chest,

Am7   A13   Am7 A13 A7♭5 A13
I never meant to make a big scene.

Am7   A13   Am7   A13
Will you resign to the latest design?

Am7   A13   Am7 A13 A7♭5 A13
You look so messy when you dress up in dreams.

Am7   A13   Am7   A13
One more for hire or a wonderful liar?

Am7   A13   Am7 A13 A7♭5 A13
I think it's time we all should come clean.

Pre-chorus 1

Am7
Stack dead actors, stacked to the rafters,

Line up the bastards, all I want is the truth.

Chorus 1

A   G
Hey, hey now, can you fake it?

F   D
Can you make it look like we want?

A   G
Hey, hey now, can you take it?

F   D
And we cry when they all die blonde.

Link 1   ‖: Am⁷ A¹³ | Am⁷ A¹³ | Am⁷ A¹³ | Am⁷ A¹³ A7♭5 A¹³ :‖

Verse 2
      Am⁷   A¹³   Am⁷
      God bless,   what a sensitive mess,
      A¹³   Am⁷   A¹³   Am⁷ A¹³ A7♭5 A¹³
      Yeah, but things aren't always what they seem.
      Am⁷   A¹³   Am⁷   A¹³
      Your teary eyes,   your famous disguise,
      Am⁷   A¹³   Am⁷ A¹³ A7♭5 A¹³
      Never knowing who to believe.
      Am⁷   A¹³   Am⁷
      See through, yeah but what do you do
      A¹³   Am⁷   A¹³   Am⁷   A¹³ A7♭5 A¹³
      When you're just another ancient drag queen?

Pre-chorus 2
      Am⁷
      Stack dead actors, stacked to the rafters,

      Line up the bastards, all I want is the truth.

Chorus 2
          A   G
      Hey, hey now, can you fake it?
             F   D
      Can you make it look like we want?
          A   G
      Hey, hey now, can you take it?
             F   D
      And we cry when they all die blonde.

Chorus 3
      A   G
      Stack dead actors, stacked to the rafters;
       F   D
      Line up all the bastards, all I want is the truth.
      A   G
      Stack dead actors, stacked to the rafters;
      F
      Line up all the bastards.
            D
      And we cry when they all die (blonde.)

Link 2 | (A) | (A) | (A) | (E♭) ‖
        blonde.

Guitar solo   ‖: A | A | A | E♭ :‖ *Play 4 times*

Chorus 4

        A   **G**
Hey, hey now, can you fake it?
            F   **D**
Can you make it look like we want?
        A   **G**
Hey, hey now, can you take it?
            F   **D**
And we cry when they all die blonde.

Chorus 5

        A   **G**
Stack dead actors, stacked to the rafters,
      F   **D**
Line up all the bastards, all I want is the truth.
A   **G**
Stack dead actors, stacked to the rafters,
      F
Line up the bastards.
        D   **N.C.**
And we cry when they all die (blonde.)

Coda | Am⁷ A¹³ | Am⁷ A¹³ | Am⁷ A¹³ | Am⁷ A¹³ |
blonde.

‖: Am⁷ A¹³ | Am⁷ A¹³ | Am⁷ A¹³ | Am⁷ A¹³ :‖ Am⁷   ‖

THE LOST ART OF KEEPING A SECRET

WORDS & MUSIC BY JOSHUA HOMME & NICK OLIVERI

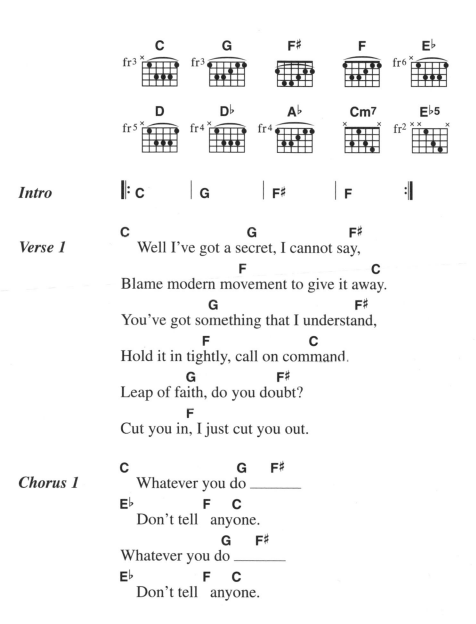

Intro
‖: C | G | F♯ | F :‖

Verse 1

C   G   F♯
Well I've got a secret, I cannot say,

                     F   C
Blame modern movement to give it away.

             G   F♯
You've got something that I understand,

             F   C
Hold it in tightly, call on command.

             G   F♯
Leap of faith, do you doubt?

             F
Cut you in, I just cut you out.

Chorus 1

C   G   F♯
Whatever you do _____

E♭   F   C
Don't tell anyone.

                G   F♯
Whatever you do _____

E♭   F   C
Don't tell anyone.

Verse 2

           G   F♯
Look for reflections in your face,
           F   C
Canine devotion, time can erase.
           G   F♯
Out on the corner, locked in your room,
           F   C
I never believe them and I never assume.
           G   F♯
Stuck in belief, there is a lie.
           F   C
Promises promise, an eye for an eye.
           G   F♯
We've got something to reveal,
           F   C
No-one can know how we feel.

Chorus 2

C   G   F♯
   Whatever you do _____
E♭   F   C
  Don't tell anyone.
            G   F♯
Whatever you do _____
E♭   F   C
  Don't tell anyone.

Chorus 3

                F♯   E♭
Whatever you do _____
D   D♭   C
  Don't tell anyone.
            G   F♯
Whatever you do _____
E♭   F   G
  Don't tell.

Bridge

F♯
  I think you already know
A♭   C
  How far I'd go not to say.
F♯
  You know the art isn't gone
A♭
  And I'm taking this song to the (grave.)

Solo | C | G | F♯ | F | C | G | F♯ | F ||
        grave.

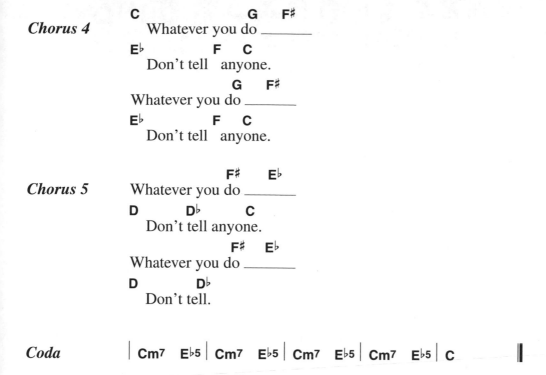

Chorus 4

C   G F♯
Whatever you do _____

E♭   F C
Don't tell anyone.

       G F♯
Whatever you do _____

E♭   F C
Don't tell anyone.

Chorus 5

       F♯ E♭
Whatever you do _____

D D♭ C
Don't tell anyone.

       F♯ E♭
Whatever you do _____

D   D♭
Don't tell.

Coda

| Cm7 E♭5 | Cm7 E♭5 | Cm7 E♭5 | Cm7 E♭5 | C   ‖

TAKE A LOOK AROUND (THEME FROM "M:I-2")

MUSIC BY LALO SCHIFRIN. WORDS BY FRED DURST

Em   G   D   C   E5 fr7   A   D5 fr5   D#5 fr6

Tune guitar down a semitone

Intro

‖: (Em)   (G) | (Em)   (D) | (Em)   (G) | (Em)   (D) :‖

‖: (Em) | (G) | (C) | (D)   :‖ *Play 3 times*

Verse 1

Em
All the teachin' in the world today,

      G
All the little girls filling up the world today.

      C
With the good comes the bad, the bad comes to good,

    D
But I'm-a gonna live my life like I should.

Em   G
    Now all the critics wanna hit it. This hit? How we did it,

                        C
Just because they don't get it, but I'll stay fitted,

                   D
New era committed, now this red cap gets a rap from his critics.

Pre-chorus

Em   G
    Do we always gotta cry, do we always gotta live inside a lie?
C
Life's just a blast, 'cause it's movin' really fast,

    D
You better stay on top or life'll kick you in the ass.

Verse 1

Em
    Follow me into a solo,

    G
Remember that kid, so what you wanna do?

     C
And where you gonna run when you're starin' down the cable

    D
Of my mic pointed at your grill like a gun?

cont.

    Em   G
Limp Bizkit is rockin' the set, it's like Russian roulette

When you're placin' your bet,

    C
So don't be upset when you're broke and you're done,

    D
'Cause I'm gonna be the one till I jet.

Chorus 1

E5   G A
I know why you wanna hate me,

E5   D5 D#5
I know why you wanna hate me,

E5   G A
I know why you wanna hate me,

        E5   D5   D#5
'Cause hate is all the world has even seen late - ly.

E5   G A
I know why you wanna hate me,

E5   D5 D#5
I know why you wanna hate me,

E5   G A
Now I know why you wanna hate me,

        E5   D5   D#5
'Cause hate is all the world has even seen late - ly.

| E5   G A | E5   D5 D#5 |

E5   G A
And now you wanna hate me,

        E5   D5   D#5
'Cause hate is all the world has even seen late - ly.

| E5   G A | E5   D5 D#5 |

E5   G A
Now you wanna hate me,

        E5   D5   D#5
'Cause hate is all the world has even seen late - ly.

Link | Em | G | C | D   ‖

Verse 3

      Em
Does anybody really know the secret

      G
Or the combination for this life

And where they keep it?

C
  It's kinda sad when you don't know the meanin'

    D
But everything happens for a reason.

Em
I don't even know what I should say,

          G
'Cause I'm an idiot, a loser, a microphone abuser.

C
  I analyse every second I exist,

D
Beatin' up my mind every second with my fist.

Pre-chorus

   Em   **G**
  And everybody wanna run, everybody wanna hide from the gun,

C
You can take a ride through this life if you want

      D
 But you can't take the edge off the knife, no sir.

Em   **G**
  And now you want your money back but you're denied,

'Cause your brains fried from the sack

C
  And there ain't nothin' I can do,

      D
'Cause life is a lesson,

You learn it when you're through.

Chorus 2

E⁵   **G A**
  I know why you wanna hate me,

E⁵   **D⁵ D♯⁵**
  I know why you wanna hate me,

E⁵   **G A**
  I know why you wanna hate me,

       E⁵   **D⁵**   **D♯⁵**
'Cause hate is all the world has even seen late - ly.

cont.

E5
   I know why you wanna hate me,   G A

E5   D5 D#5
   I know why you wanna hate me,

E5   G A
   Now I know why you wanna hate me,

               E5   D5   D#5
'Cause hate is all the world has even seen late - ly.

| E5 | G A | E5 | D5 D#5 |

E5   G A
   Now you wanna hate me,

               E5   D5   D#5
'Cause hate is all the world has even seen late - ly.

| E5 | G A | E5 | D5 D#5 |

E5   G A
   Now you wanna hate me,

               E5   D5   D#5
'Cause hate is all the world has even seen late - ly.

Bridge   ‖: E5   G A | E5   D5 D#5 :‖ *Play 6 times*

               ‖: Em | G | C | D :‖ *Play 4 times*
               Now   I   know   why,

Chorus 3

E5   G A
Now I know why you wanna hate me,

E5   D5 D#5
Now I know why you wanna hate me,

E5   G A
Now I know why you wanna hate me,

               E5   D5   D#5   E5
'Cause hate is all the world has even seen late - ly,

G A   E5   D5   D#5   E5
    'Cause hate is all the world has even seen late - ly,

G A   E5   D5   D#5
    'Cause hate is all the world has even seen late - ly.

Coda   ‖: Em | G | C | D :‖ *Repeat and fade*

TEENAGE DIRTBAG

WORDS & MUSIC BY BRENDAN BROWN

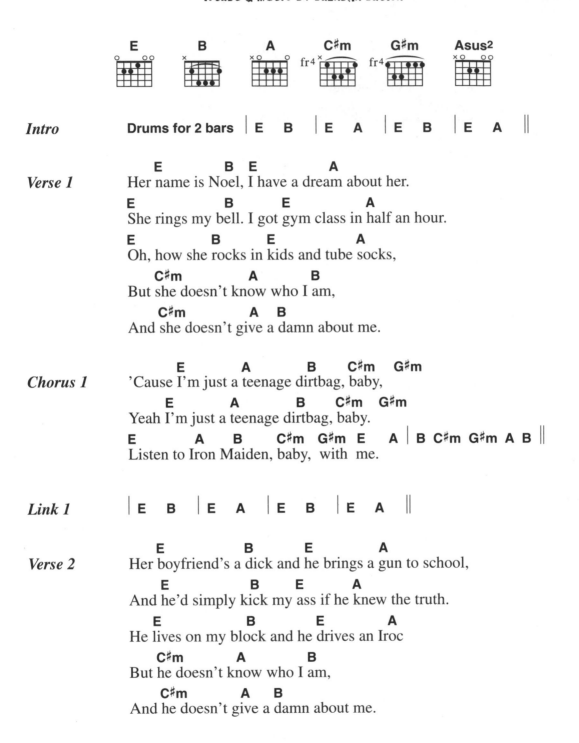

Intro Drums for 2 bars | E B | E A | E B | E A ‖

Verse 1
```
          E        B  E              A
Her name is Noel, I have a dream about her.
E            B      E            A
She rings my bell. I got gym class in half an hour.
E           B       E            A
Oh, how she rocks in kids and tube socks,
    C#m            A        B
But she doesn't know who I am,
    C#m            A  B
And she doesn't give a damn about me.
```

Chorus 1
```
              E      A      B   C#m  G#m
'Cause I'm just a teenage dirtbag, baby,
              E      A      B   C#m  G#m
Yeah I'm just a teenage dirtbag, baby.
E           A  B      C#m  G#m E   A | B C#m G#m A B ‖
Listen to Iron Maiden, baby,  with  me.
```

Link 1 | E B | E A | E B | E A ‖

Verse 2
```
          E        B      E            A
Her boyfriend's a dick and he brings a gun to school,
      E          B      E            A
And he'd simply kick my ass if he knew the truth.
      E         B      E            A
He lives on my block and he drives an Iroc
    C#m            A        B
But he doesn't know who I am,
    C#m            A  B
And he doesn't give a damn about me.
```

Chorus 2   As Chorus 1

Bridge
     E Asus²   E Asus²   E Asus²
         Oh yeah, _____ dirtbag, _____
      C♯m   G♯m   A   B
No, she doesn't know what she's missing,
     E Asus²   E Asus²   E Asus²
         Oh yeah, _____ dirtbag, _____
      C♯m   G♯m   A   B
No, she doesn't know what she's missing.

Link 2 | E   B | E   A ||

Verse 3
        E   B   E   A
Man, I feel like mould, it's prom night and I am lonely.
E   B   E   A
Low and behold, she's walking over to me.
E   B   E   A
This must be fake, my lip starts to shake.
C♯m   A   B
How does she know who I am?
   C♯m   A   B
And why does she give a damn about?

Chorus 3
        E   A   B   C♯m   G♯m
I've got two tickets to Iron Maiden, baby,
E   A   B   C♯m   G♯m
Come with me Friday, don't say maybe.
E   A   B   C♯m G♯m E   A | B C♯m G♯m A B ||
I'm just a teenage dirtbag, baby, like   you.

Coda
     E Asus²   E Asus²   E Asus²
         Oh yeah, _____ dirtbag, _____
      C♯m   G♯m   A   B
No, she doesn't know what she's missing,
     E Asus²   E Asus²   E Asus²
         Oh yeah, _____ dirtbag, _____
      C♯m   G♯m   A   E   B   E   A
No, she doesn't know what she's mis - sing, yeah. _____

    | E   B | E | A G♯m F♯m | E   ‖

TOO MANY DJS

WORDS & MUSIC BY STEPHEN DEWAELE & DAVID DEWAELE

E5   Em   C   G   A   C#sus2   G#7

F#m7add11   B7add11   E   C#m   D   F   Esus4   Eadd♭5

Intro   ‖: E5   Em | E5   Em | E5   Em | E5   Em :‖   *Play 3 times*

Verse 1

N.C.   E5   Em
Everybody wants to be the DJ,
E5
Everybody thinks that it's oh so easy.
               C
You think you belong and you come on strong,
      G   A   E5   Em
But I can still tell the right from the wrong.

Verse 2

N.C.   E5   Em
I could never be that kind of girl,
E5
Nobody takes the time to turn.
          C
You always act as if it's understood,
      G   A   Em7
But sweet revenge is finger-lickin' good.

Pre-chorus 1

               C#sus2   G#7
But if only I could sell myself
               F#m7add11   B7add11
The way that even I would buy,
          C#sus2   G#7
If only I could sell myself
               F#m7add11   B7add11
The way that even I would buy.

Chorus 1

  E⁵   **C**   **C♯m**
   Something's gotta give, something's gotta give,

    D **F** **E⁵**
I don't know. _____

         C   **C♯m**
Something's gotta give, something's gotta give,

    D   **E⁵**
I don't know. _____

Verse 3

  E⁵
Here's one thing how to understand me,

Loneliness tastes like cotton candy.

  C
You answer "I love you" with "I know,"

  G   **A**   **Em⁷**
You never check the messages on your answer-phone.

Pre-chorus 2 As Pre-chorus 1

Chorus 2

  E⁵   **C**   **C♯m**
   Something's gotta give, something's gotta give,

    D **F** **E⁵**
I don't know. _____

         C   **C♯m**
Something's gotta give, something's gotta give,

I don't (know.)

D **F**	**E⁵**	**E⁵**	**E⁵**	**E⁵**	‖ **Sound effects** ‖

know. _____

Instrumental ‖: **E⁵** | **E⁵** | **E⁵** **G** | **G** **E⁵** :‖ *Play 4 times*

        ‖: **E** | **Esus⁴** | **Eadd♭5** | **E⁵** :‖ *Play 4 times*

Chorus 3

  E⁵   **C**   **C♯m**
   Something's gotta give, something's gotta give,

    D **F** **E⁵**
I don't know. _____

         C   **C♯m**
Something's got to give, something's got to give,

    D   **F**
I don't know. _____

THE TREES

WORDS & MUSIC BY JARVIS COCKER, NICK BANKS, CANDIDA DOYLE, STEPHEN MACKEY, MARK WEBBER, STANLEY MYERS & HAL SHAPER

F#maj7   G#m/C#   G#m7/F#   F#   B   C#m

Intro

‖: F#maj7 | F#maj7   G#m/C# :‖

Verse 1

F#maj7
   I took an air rifle,
G#m/C# F#maj7   G#m/C#
Shot   a magpie to the ground
F#maj7 G#m7/F#   F#maj7 G#m/C#
   And it died without a sound.
F#maj7
   Your skin's so pale
      G#m/C# F#maj7   G#m/C#
Against the   fallen autumn leaves.
G#m7/F#   F#maj7
   And no-one saw us but the trees.

Chorus 1

      F#   F#maj7
Yeah, the trees, those useless trees
        B   F#maj7
Produce the air that I am breathing.
     F#   F#maj7
Yeah, the trees, those useless trees,
       B G#m/C#   F#maj7   G#m/C#
They never said that you were leaving.

Verse 2

F#maj7
   I carved your name
     G#m/C# F#maj7   G#m/C#
With a   heart just up above,
G#m7/F#
   Now swollen, distorted,
     F#maj7   G#m/C#
Unrecognisable, like our love.

cont.

F#maj7
  The smell of leaf mould

  G#m/C# F#maj7   G#m/C#
And the   sweetness of decay

G#m7/F#   F#maj7
  Are the incense at the funeral procession here today.

  G#m/C# F#   F#maj7
Chorus 2 In   the trees, those useless trees

       B   F#maj7
Produce the air that I am breathing.

      F#   F#maj7
Yeah, the trees, those useless trees,

      B G#m/C#   F#maj7
They never said that you were leaving.

  B
Bridge You try to shape the world to what you want the world to be,

Carving your name a thousand times

              C#
Won't bring you back to me. ⸻

  F#maj7
Oh, no, I might as well,

             G#m/C# F#maj7 G#m/C#
I might as well go tell it to   the trees.

Link ‖: F#maj7 | F#maj7 G#m/C# :‖

   ‖: (F#maj7) | (F#maj7) (G#m/C#) :‖ *Play 6 times*

   ‖: F#maj7 | F#maj7 G#m/C# :‖ *Play 4 times*

   G#m/C# F#   F#maj7
Chorus 3 Oh yeah, the   trees, those useless trees

       B   F#maj7
Produce the air that I am breathing.

      F#   F#maj7
Yeah, the trees, those useless trees,

      B G#m/C#   F#maj7
They never said that you were leaving.

         G#m/C# F#maj7
Coda ‖: Go and tell it to   the trees, yeah. :‖ *Play 5 times*

UNTITLED
WORDS & MUSIC BY BILLY CORGAN

Bsus⁴   Aadd⁹   E   Bsus²   G#m♮6   F#7add¹¹

Tune guitar down one semitone

Verse 1

Bsus⁴
Should I know what I'm missing?

What's to stop? Look and listen.
Aadd⁹   E   Bsus⁴
Feel love, to be in love around.

Verse 2

Bsus⁴
Anyone can hold a promise,

Not everyone can feel honoured.
Aadd⁹   E   Bsus⁴
To be in love, to feel love around.

Chorus 1

E   Bsus²   Aadd⁹
Turn me on, give me speech.
E   Bsus²   Aadd⁹
Let me be what I need,
E
You're enough for (me.)

Link 1

| Bsus⁴ | Bsus⁴ | Bsus⁴ | Bsus⁴ ‖
me.

Bridge

Bsus⁴
Many times while you sleep

I'm dreaming of what to keep.

You know your wish, hold it true,

To slay the things that trouble you.

Chorus 2

G#m♮6   A   E
Turn me on, out of reach. _____

G#m♮6   A   E
Listen here, feel me. _____

G#m♮6   Aadd9   Bsus4
Just believe, just believe you'll see.

      Aadd9   E
To feel love, to be in love a - (round.)

Solo

| F#7add11 | F#7add11 | F#7add11 | F#7add11 ‖
- round.

Verse 3

Badd4
Hold the truth if you want it,

If you don't I will flaunt it.

     Aadd9   E   Bsus4
To feel love, to be in love around.

Verse 4

Bsus4
When you're young you can promise

Anything that you wanted,

     Aadd9   E   Bsus4
To be in love, to feel love around.

Chorus 3

Aadd9   E   Bsus4
Turn me on, let me speak _____

Aadd9   E   Bsus4
From my heart, I will see. _____

     Aadd9   E   Bsus4
Bring happiness, just happiness for you and me.

     Aadd9   E   Bsus4
To feel love, to be in love around.

     Aadd9   E   Bsus4
To be love, to feel love around.

     Aadd9   E   Bsus4
To feel love, to be in love around.

     Aadd9   E   Bsus4
To be love, to feel love around.

Link 2

‖: Bsus4 | Bsus4 | Aadd9 E :‖

Coda

Bsus⁴
I know your wish, I hold it true

Aadd⁹   E   Bsus⁴
{ (Feel love all around).
        To hide the things that trouble you

Aadd⁹   E   Bsus⁴
{ (Feel love all around).
        Turn me on, out of reach

Aadd⁹   E   Bsus⁴
{ (Feel love all around).
        Let me speak of my peace

Aadd⁹   E   Bsus⁴
{ (Feel love all around).
        Draw from me what you need

Aadd⁹   E   Bsus⁴
{ (Feel love all around).
        You'll never hate or hurry me

Aadd⁹   E   Bsus⁴
(Feel love all around).

Aadd⁹   E   Bsus⁴
‖: (To feel love, to be in love around.) :‖   *Play 5 times*
With solo ad lib.